Between Sun and Sod

Between Sun and Sod

AN INFORMAL HISTORY OF THE TEXAS PANHANDLE

by WILLIE NEWBURY LEWIS

Illustrations by H. D. BUGBEE

Introduction by FRED RATHJEN

TEXAS A&M UNIVERSITY PRESS *College Station*

Library of Congress Cataloging in Publication Data

Lewis, Willie Newbury.
    Between sun and sod.

    Rev. ed. of a work originally published in 1938.
    Bibliography: p.
    Includes index.
    1. Texas Panhandle—History. 2. Frontier and
pioneer life—Texas Panhandle. 3. Cattle trade—Texas
Panhandle. I. Title.
F392.P168L48 1976   976.4'8   75-40893
ISBN 0-89096-010-0

Manufactured in the United States of America
Revised edition

Dedicated, with respect and affection, to those grand old men who in their youth were the cowboys that made the West—and to my husband who was the finest cowboy of them all.

Contents

Introduction

WHEN the United States observed its Centennial, the Texas Panhandle remained a part of a substantially unoccupied corridor in the interior of the country lying roughly between the 99th and 104th meridians. Though anything but unknown to Anglo-Americans, this corridor simply did not attract settlement, because until the mid-seventies there were more desirable areas to be had. By about 1875, however, there was not much left and those who wished to cash in on the last of the free land bonanzas of the American frontier had to take the less desirable portions of the continent. But occupying and using land is considerably more than merely wanting it, and the Anglo-American frontiersman was ill equipped in institutions, tools, and thought patterns to appropriate to his use the sub-humid plains of North America. Roughly a decade before the first permanently domiciled Anglo-Americans arrived in the Panhandle, however, far-removed circumstances led them to develop an institution that would open the area to settlement and would distinguish itself as perhaps the most environmentally harmonious institution white men have applied in the Great Plains: the Cattle Kingdom.

The Cattle Kingdom is certainly one of the best known, albeit one of the least understood, phases of the American experience. By 1876 it was well established economically and methodologically and was quickly appropriating the unoccupied grasslands of the continent. The arrival of Anglo-American cattlemen in the Panhandle in 1876 occurred naturally and in the logical sequence of broader historic evolution. But it marked a break with the long-term history of the region, and in fact the New Mexican sheepmen who came at about the same time and remained but a short while were far more within the Panhandle's historic and cultural traditions. The cattlemen were indeed pioneers from the Anglo-American perspective, but not by the measure through which the Texas Panhandle dates human history.

The earliest evidence of man's presence in the southern plains is found in the Folsom and Clovis projectile points left by the big game hunters who roamed the region at least as long ago as 12,000 years. These ancient plainsmen found an environment rich in Pleistocene wildlife, sustained themselves upon the great Columbian mammoths and ancient buffalo, *bison antiquus*, and began man's agonizing climb toward organized society. By the end of the prehistoric period, the Panhandle aborigines had evolved into the horticultural town-dwellers who lived along the Canadian River and its tributaries and are known to modern scholars as Antelope Creek Focus. For about a century and a half this culture flourished only to disappear rather suddenly about the middle of the fifteenth century. Its fate and the reasons for it are unclear, but probably the arrival of Athapaskan nomads who were to become the historic Apaches had something to do with it. In any case, when the expedition of Francisco Vasquez de Coronado visited the Texas Panhandle in 1541, the towns of Antelope Creek Focus were not found, but the observations of that expedition establish clearly the presence of the Apaches in the southern plains.

By the middle of the sixteenth century, the Apaches had evidently evolved well-developed culture patterns that were to endure among the Plains tribes for as long as the aboriginal Americans were free to live independently in the region. That is, they were nomadic hunters who subsisted almost exclusively upon the buffalo, deriving food, shelter, clothing, and many incidentals of life from the bison herds. To put it another way, the aboriginal plainsmen adapted to the circumstances of nature and sought their cultural destiny within nature's framework—perhaps

because of native good judgment, perhaps because they lacked the technology to do otherwise. In any case, the early Apaches found the Panhandle an attractive place, for it was rich in buffalo, relatively mild in climate, and, after the Spaniards colonized the river valleys of New Mexico, close to the source of the horses that turned the plodding life-style of pedestrian nomads into a brilliant culture of horse nomads. The enormous attractiveness of the southern plains, in fact, brought the Comanches sweeping into the area from the north. About 1700 these Shoshone-speaking Indians, formerly of the mountains, literally rode into the history of Texas; they dispossessed the Apaches, sending them scurrying across the Southwest in fragmented bands, made the plains south of the Arkansas River their homeland, and held them successfully against all comers until they were eventually overwhelmed almost two centuries later by the technologically and numerically superior Anglo-Americans.

The Spaniards, who, with their own arid-land heritage, should have occupied the plains and held them, never did so. As highly successful explorers, the Spaniards traveled over West Texas as they pleased, knew virtually every place of significance, and enriched the land with their place names. In the earlier days of Spanish conquest when only they had horses and the Plains tribes were afoot, the

Spaniards found nothing in West Texas to make occupation worth their while. Decades later, when the Plains Indians had acquired horses and become superb horsemen, scourging the frontiers of New Spain, the Spaniards had plenty of reason to want to conquer them. By that time, however, conquest and occupation of the area east of the Pecos was far beyond the Spaniards' grasp. The important point, however, is that beginning with the Coronado *entrada* the whole of western Texas was oriented toward the Spanish Southwest and was a part of New Mexico in the Spanish concept of their own American dominions. And if the Spaniards did not occupy the southern plains, they never lost their knowledge of the region and of how to travel through it. Throughout Spanish times and down to the last moment before the Anglo-American occupation, the cultural descendants of Spaniards continued to travel through the region at will, to go where they pleased, and to trade with the Indians according to the needs of both parties.

Early in the nineteenth century a process of reorientation of the Panhandle toward the east set in, a process that would eventually dispossess both the Indians and Hispanic people and claim the region for English speakers. Initiated by various impulses—partly commercial expansion, partly desire to know what was in the west, partly imperialism— American thrusts westward brought exploratory groups across the Panhandle.

Eighteen hundred twenty-one marks a fairly precise date for the beginning of this reorientation, since in that year the expedition of Major Stephen H. Long explored the Panhandle along the Canadian River. The records of the Long expedition contain the first systematic examination of the Panhandle, and the expedition initiated the scientific exploration of the region by the United States government. This process was to continue through several expeditions and conclude with the Pacific railroad surveys in 1853. About fifteen years after Long passed through the Canadian River valley, the dour Santa Fe trader Josiah Gregg traveled eastward below the south bank of the Canadian. Gregg described the route in his widely read *Commerce of the Prairies*, and in the summer of 1849 Captain Randolph B. Marcy precisely marked it as the Fort Smith–Santa Fe Trail, which carried perhaps two thousand California-bound argonauts during that summer. All these factors combined to pull the Panhandle away from its historic moorings in New Mexico, and the region's reorientation toward Anglo-America was assured politically in 1850 when the Compromise measures fixed regional boundaries so as to include the Panhandle in a political entity centered far to the southeast.

In summary, before the Civil War the Canadian River valley and the Red River valley and the major tributaries of that stream had been explored, and one well-known trail—the Fort Smith–Santa Fe Trail—had been clearly marked and heavily used. And only shortly before the Civil War, a practical railroad route had been mapped across the region. Thus the region was well known to the government and could have been well known to any person who knew to consult government documents. Except for a few informed persons, however, this knowledge of the region remained largely untouched, offering far more fascination for twentieth-century historians than it did guidance for nineteenth-century settlers.

Following the Civil War the Panhandle region remained briefly outside the interest of white settlers or of the government, but the events of westward expansion soon brought the region to both private and public attention. The buffalo of the Great Plains had for hundreds of years sustained the Indians of the region, but except for a limited robe trade, they did not excite the interest of white men until the early 1870's, when successful experiments in tanning buffalo hides created a demand, and the race to the buffalo range was on. The Texas Panhandle was one of the richest hunting grounds the hide hunters ever found. Despite the commonly held belief that the Pan-

handle was prohibited to white hunters because of the Medicine Lodge treaties of 1867, they invaded the region in force in 1874. Their effects were twofold: the buffalo perished apace and the Indians were outraged. Already restive, the southern plains tribes found the destruction of their mainstay intolerable, and, under the leadership of two young men, Isatai, the medicine man, and Quanah Parker, the war chief, they plotted and launched an attack upon the hunters' post, Adobe Walls. Although intended as the first step in rolling back the white tide, the battle at Adobe Walls turned out to be the first stanza in the Indians' swan song, for it firmed the government's will to launch a campaign of pacification against the tribes of the southern plains. The Red River War resulted.

Peculiarly, the Red River War has attracted little public attention and not a great deal from professional historians. The campaign was extensive, well planned, well executed, and the soldiers involved let their work speak for itself. Good soldiering, like sound scholarship or great artistry, stands on its merit and no amount of showmanship makes greatness of mediocrity—except, of course, to those who do not know the difference in the first place. Although the late summer and early fall of 1874 were sweltering and the late fall and winter days of that year unbelievably cold, the campaigns of the Red River War had by January, 1875, cleared the Panhandle region of almost all hostile Indians—Comanches, Kiowas, Cheyennes, and Arapahoes—and the last holdouts gave up without further resistance by summer. To ensure the victory thus won, the government placed Fort Elliott on Sweetwater Creek just west of the 100th meridian. As events turned out, Fort Elliott served far less to confine Indians than to subsidize and support the occupation of the region by whites.

Early in 1876, then, the stage was set for the easy appropriation of the Panhandle by white people: the Indians had been removed and the buffalo cleared to make way for cattle and eventually for the plow; Fort Elliott stood prepared to aid and support an influx of civilian population; and, almost as if entering on cue, the first cattlemen drove their herds onto the rich pasturage of the region late in the year. Mobeetie, originally a buffalo hunters' "Hidetown," developed into the mother city of the Panhandle under the shadow of Fort Elliott and in response to the needs of both the military post and the surrounding ranches for goods and services. A quickly felt need for legal and political institutions was met in 1879 with the organization of Wheeler County, the first organized political unit in the Panhandle.

Tascosa, about a hundred miles west of Mobeetie, grew

from a little group of New Mexican sheepmen who settled along the Canadian in the western Panhandle late in 1876, and developed as a commercial response to the demands of an evolving ranching economy. Clarendon, the third of the original trio of Panhandle towns, differs from her sister communities in that she was consciously promoted.

Although Mobeetie, Tascosa, and Clarendon were not destined to amount to much in the great scheme of American development or, for that matter, to have long-standing significance as urban or commercial centers of the Panhandle region, their study remains important to an understanding of the region and ultimately to the comprehensive history of the larger entities of state and nation.

Introduction xiii

The English have long understood the importance of local history as the basic unit from which larger history is woven, and their historians have not considered local history unworthy of their time or too elementary for their consideration. On the contrary, while working toward the great sweep of imperial history, they have known that its fundamentals are in the towns and counties of the realm. Perforce localities in England have greater historical depth than do those of America, and no one argues that local history anywhere is as grand as the Roman Empire, or as exotic as the French Revolution, or, in the English-speaking world, as darkly, fascinatingly tragic as Russia.

On the other hand, local history enjoys certain advantages not common to more complex units. Sources are ordinarily near at hand and, especially in the American West, persons are available who at least know the land intimately and occasionally one finds and may interview those who participated in events long past. Moreover, in almost any social entity, one finds mankind in microcosm and hence more susceptible of examination, analysis, and eventual generalization—with, of course, a scrupulous regard for confining one's generalizations to those the available evidence supports.

Local history, moreover, provides a natural channel for introducing youth to the historian's discipline and to their American heritage. Few youth have the opportunity, and perhaps even the motivation, to dig into the bedrock of national history, but what is known and commonplace —that is, what the individual may personally identify with —provides access to history in a primary sense and usually an opportunity to approach it through primary sources. To put it another way, local history provides a unique opportunity to tap the natural inquisitiveness of youth and to direct it along constructive channels. It was in precisely this way, in fact, that the prehistoric ruins known to contemporary archaeologists as Antelope Creek Focus were discovered. In 1907 a bright, curious lad persuaded a teacher who was alert to the inquiries of students to take him and other youngsters to look at ruins of a "buried city" that were thought to be the remains of a forgotten Spanish settlement. The ruins turned out to predate the arrival of Europeans in the New World by a considerable time and to be those of a unique prehistoric culture. The youngster in question, the late Floyd V. Studer, devoted a lifetime to excavation, study, locating, and mapping the sites that make up Antelope Creek Focus.

But if local history is notable for its potential, it is also notable for its pitfalls. Like the work of bibliographers and genealogists, the local historian's work is preeminently a labor of love, and therein lies the trap. As in other areas of human endeavor, emotional involvement often distorts vision, and when the local historian is blinded to the extent that he produces chauvinism, the purposes of history are not served. Perhaps, therefore, as in no other field, the rules of scholarship must be rigidly adhered to in local history.

Maybe because its history is relatively short in terms of Anglo-American occupation, Texas Panhandle history has received considerable attention, and its people have shown an intelligent interest in their past. In the late 1920's many of the region's pioneers were still living, and the younger members of Panhandle society were consequently in very close touch with their region's history. Accordingly, when the Panhandle-Plains Historical Society was organized in the early twenties, it found ready support among those who had participated in the region's pioneer experience and among second- and third-generation West Texans as well. As a matter of fact, the society was organized through the vision and leadership of Miss Hattie M. Anderson, a youthful professor of history at West Texas State Normal College and a transplanted Missourian. Its charter membership was composed of faculty and students from "the Normal," as the institution was commonly called. Soon members of the dormant Panhandle-Plains Old Settlers Association joined the youthful group,

and the society had its first annual meeting on February 24, 1922. Immediately, the work of collecting and preserving both the artifacts and documents of Panhandle-Plains history was begun, and soon the nucleus of what was to become the Panhandle-Plains Historical Museum was gathered.

Volume I of the *Panhandle-Plains Historical Review* appeared in 1928 and emerged quickly as an outstanding journal of regional history. The first issue published articles by Professor L. F. Sheffy, Miss Anderson, and J. Evetts Haley; the cover of volume II featured the first of thirty-four ink drawings by the great regional artist, Harold Bugbee, which were to appear on the covers of the *Review*. In volumes II and III, articles by Walter Prescott Webb presaged the publication of his epic work, *The Great Plains*, which was to appear in 1931. Through the 1930's, Sheffy and Haley contributed regularly to the *Review*, but other authors whose names were well known, or about to become so, appeared, including W. C. Holden, who remains a leading student of both the history and archaeology of West Texas; Angie Debo, who pioneered the field of Indian history long before it became fashionable; Rupert N. Richardson and C. C. Rister, who emerged as leading scholars of Texas and the Southwest; Floyd V. Studer and C. Stuart Johnston, who probed deeply and wrote of the prehistory of the Panhandle-Plains region; C. Boone McClure, who became director of the Panhandle-Plains Historical Museum and held that post until his recent retirement; and H. Bailey Carroll, who became an expert on southwestern trails and served for many years as director of the Texas State Historical Association and editor of its journal, *The Southwestern Historical Quarterly.*

In fact, the first few issues of the *Panhandle-Plains Historical Review* would seem almost to have touched off an explosion of investigation into Panhandle-Plains history by a number of talented persons. The quiet, thorough scholarship of L. F. Sheffy eventually produced *The Life and Times of Timothy Dwight Hobart* (1950) and *The Francklyn Land and Cattle Company* (1963), while the appearance of Evetts Haley's *XIT Ranch of Texas* (1929) and *Charles Goodnight* (1936) graced regional historical literature with a rare literary eloquence. Undoubtedly the hard times of the 1930's inhibited much useful enterprise of many different kinds, but the Depression was not entirely disastrous for some aspects of regional history, since the Federal Writers Program of the Works Progress Administration encouraged and subsidized much worthwhile investigation into local history in the region. But the study of regional prehistory probably benefited most because of a dynamic, young paleontologist at what had now become West Texas State College. C. Stuart Johnston enjoyed a Midas touch in his applications for federal funding, and, backed with WPA money, he scoured the Panhandle for significant fossil deposits and then organized highly systematic excavations that accumulated a collection of fossil specimens of real scientific importance. Meanwhile, Floyd V. Studer continued his studies of Panhandle prehistory with emphasis upon the excavation of Antelope Creek Focus sites. Both men published their findings in the pages of the *Review.*

The growing archival collections of the Panhandle-Plains Historical Society supported an increasing amount of more specifically academic inquiry into regional topics as Professors Sheffy and Anderson and their younger colleague, Dr. Ima C. Barlow, sent students into the society's collections to write an imposing number of really sound master's theses that explored county history, ranch history, and a diversity of other topics relating to the Texas Panhandle. A number of these found their way into print in the pages of the *Review*, or occasionally in book form, as in the case of John McCarty's *Maverick Town: The Story of Old Tascosa* (1946). Other persons perhaps unknowingly gathered regional history in other ways. Fascinated by the recollections of XIT cowboys, Cordia Sloan Duke goaded them into relating their stories so that she could record them. Years later, under the editorial guidance of Joe B. Frantz, Mrs. Duke's interviews appeared as *Six Thousand Miles of Fence: Life on the XIT Ranch of Texas* (1961).

So despite drought and depression, the 1930's were an exciting decade for regional history, and it is worth noting that a large portion of the responsible persons were women. There was, therefore, a certain naturalness in the publication of Willie Newbury Lewis's *Between Sun and Sod* in 1938. Unfortunately, the book never achieved the recognition it should have had and never took its proper place in the body of contemporaneous regional literature. The first printing was marred by numerous editorial and mechanical defects and was at once removed from the market. A second small printing sold out quickly, whereupon copies of the first, flawed printing, which Mrs. Lewis believed to have been destroyed, began to appear. Mrs. Lewis and her husband went to court to stop its further distribution.

Mrs. Lewis's interest in the Panhandle, its people, and especially in her own family's experiences in the region continued, however, and led eventually to the writing of *Tapadero* (1972), a biography of her rancher husband, William J. Lewis. Public acceptance of *Tapadero* and requests from readers for *Between Sun and Sod* rekindled

Mrs. Lewis's interest in the earlier regional study. The present edition of *Between Sun and Sod* has been largely rewritten and revised, the narrative tightened by the removal of some peripheral material from the original text to an appendix, and the bibliography verified, expanded, and put into a technically proper form in order to make it more useful to researchers. Fortunately, through the efforts of Mrs. Olive Bugbee, Harold Bugbee's original illustrations have been located and are reproduced in the new edition.

Inasmuch as the actual occupation of the Panhandle by Anglo-American people coincided with the United States' Centennial observance, the publication of this new edition of *Between Sun and Sod* is a timely and appropriate contribution to the United States Bicentennial–Panhandle Centennial observance.

Although generally concerned with the free grass era in the Texas Panhandle—and, in a highly personal, informal way, a history of the region—Mrs. Lewis's focus is on Clarendon, one of the three original Panhandle towns from which settlement, economic development, and especially political organization emanated. Unlike her sister settlements, Mobeetie and Tascosa, which developed as a consequence of some other activity, Clarendon was planned and actively promoted as both a business venture and a utopian community. Its original population was much more homogeneous (exclusively Anglo and Methodist), more educated, cultured, and certainly more purposefully moral than that commonly found in frontier towns, and the community displayed the kinds of traits, both good and bad, that organized morality ordinarily produces. Much of the American story is one of men modifying, or trying to modify, both conditions and mankind to suit their own concept of what the scheme of things ought to be. Clarendon's story is a pointed example. But if that community's story is one of men establishing themselves and righteousness upon the frontier, it is also a story of a frontier modifying people and their community. Therefore, as a study in social evolution in a frontier environment, Clarendon's experience is illuminating because, although its leaders did maintain their rigidly structured ideal for a time, the community could not retain for long the utopian characteristics its founders expected to establish forever.

In 1912, when Willie Lewis came to the Panhandle to live, the region had pretty well emerged from the early phases of development, but it remained rich in the presence of people, customs, and ways of its pioneer period. Fascinated by what she saw around her, the young woman recognized historical significance when she saw it, observed carefully, and remembered well. Ultimately, her fascination produced *Between Sun and Sod*.

Between Sun and Sod makes no pretense of being "professional" history. Rather, like much really good local history, it is the product of an intelligent, non-professional motivated by curiosity, ties of kinship, and attachment to the region. It falls somewhere between history in a more or less formal sense of that term and personal narrative, and precisely to these motivations the work owes both its value and charm. Obviously the author knew well many of the persons who participated in the events of which she writes, though she was herself about a generation removed from them in time. Most importantly, Willie Lewis seems to have understood by instinct what others spend years in graduate schools trying to learn: the nature and importance of primary materials. Accordingly, she sought out persons who had participated in the events of the regional past, got their stories through correspondence when necessary, but personally interviewed them when possible—long before the technique was systematized, popularized, and glamorized as oral history. In the process she accumulated a comparatively modest but significant collection of documents that illuminate the regional story and are certainly worthy of preservation.

Mrs. Lewis's perspective is strongly romantic but not

saccharine, her view of people realistic but tolerant and level-headed. One suspects that few people fooled her and that local myth beclouded neither her vision nor thinking, for she saw cattle barons as not necessarily greater men than shopkeepers and preachers as not necessarily better than cowhands. And indeed the charm and perhaps the greatest significance of *Between Sun and Sod* come through in its revelations of the perceptions and reactions of a sensitive, intelligent, and cultured person to Clarendon's immediate past as the Panhandle emerged from its frontier era.

FRED RATHJEN

Preface

Between Sun and Sod was written many years ago. Its beginning arose from a desire to preserve for the children a permanent record of their father's early life on the Panhandle Plains. However, as my interest and understanding of the subject increased, I came to realize that the story of my husband and the story of the region were closely related, and that, for the sake of coherence, his story should be preceded by the story of the land which produced him.

No effort was made to write history in its more accepted or academic form, but simply to reproduce the scene by describing with accuracy the character of the land and of the people who lived upon it, their mode of daily life, their customs and mores. Civilization marches upward by decisive steps, and a certain type of individual is required to make each step possible. Opening a new land is always accomplished by men who are hardy, physically strong, fearless, unrestrained, both self-confident and self-determined. The buffalo hunters were men of this kind. After them came the soldier and the cowboy, who had many of the same traits of character. The cowboy's presence, however, made possible the formation of an organized mode of livelihood in the Panhandle. Following the cowboy came a more settled and family-oriented type, the men who demanded law and order as a protection for their families and schools and churches for the training of their children. Such were the pioneers who changed the frontier to the Panhandle of today.

Emphasis was placed on Clarendon largely because, as the home of my husband, it afforded me the easiest access to events of the past, but also because of the character of the colony which was established, according to its founder, to bring Methodism, education, and temperance to the frontier. Even though the minister himself failed to abide by his principles, the mere suggestion of their presence attracted a superior type of settler. By the end of the era, Tascosa was known as the "capital of the free grass era," Mobeetie as the home of frontier law, and Clarendon as the Christian colony.

I wish to thank the many people whose cooperation made my book possible, particularly the entire staff of the

Panhandle-Plains Historical Museum; Mrs. Fred Chamberlain, who patiently rode the plains with me for four years through dust storms, northers, and heat in search of data; Mrs. Marguerite Goodner, formerly of the Clarendon High School; my brother Dr. Edward Newbury of the Department of Psychology at the University of Kentucky; and Mr. Victor White, who served as advisor and critic.

WILLIE NEWBURY LEWIS

"Strong sun across the sod can make such quickening . . ."
"Song for the Passing of a Beautiful Woman"
in *The American Rhythm*, by Mary Austin

CHAPTER I

Prologue

(The Wilderness and the Indian)

In the extreme northwestern part of Texas lies the region known as the Panhandle. To the west of it is New Mexico; to the east and north, Oklahoma; and across its southern portion meander the muddy waters of the Prairie Dog Town Fork of the Red River, the great Rio Roxo, along the banks of which warring Comanches and Kiowas once camped, and across which, in times gone by, thousands of cattle were driven on their way north to market.

The westernmost portion is a broad tableland of perfectly flat country, through which the Canadian River cuts the gorge that divides the North and South Plains.[1] Chiefly because of climate and the resultant agriculture, the Plains are divided into the North Plains, the North Central Plains, and the South Plains. The North Central Plains

of Texas are an extension into Texas of the lower level of the Great Plains, which extend northward to the Canadian border, paralleling the Great High Plains to the west.[2] The North Central Plains of Texas extend from the blackland belt on the east to the cap rock escarpment on the west. From north to south they extend from the Red River to the Colorado. Forming their eastern edge are the ridges and canyons of the escarpment which forms the cap rock or "breaks" of the plains. Like a rampart, the cap rock shelters the fertile, rolling prairies that lie below. It is a high, broad belt, halfway between desert and woodland, a part of the plateau that stretches from Texas to Wyoming. Together with the majestic Rockies, which rise high on the west, and the Mississippi River, which flows far below, it cuts the United States in two.

It is a region low in rainfall and only raggedly carpeted with grass, where overcrowding herds have long since tramped dry the lakes and destroyed the lush green

---

[1] See map, "Major Natural Regions of Texas," *Texas Almanac, 1966–1967*, p. 338.

[2] The Great Plains area, as Walter Prescott Webb defined it, "does not conform in its boundaries to those commonly given by geographers and historians. The Great Plains comprise a much greater area than is usually designated—an area which may best be defined in terms of topography, vegetation, and rainfall" (*The Great Plains*, p. 3). See also the relief map of the High Plains (p. 15), which shows the area from the Pecos River in Texas to the Platte River in Wyoming and Nebraska.

grass that once grew stirrup-high along the creeks, where the plough has torn out the friendly grass roots so ideally suited to hold the soil and has allowed the wind to have its way.[3]

But in times gone by, before the coming of the white race, before the plough had altered the climate, it was an abundant and extravagant land, where Nature supplied food and water in plenty for both man and beast, where year followed year in unbelievable contrast and the seasons completed their cycle with scorching suns and blinding snows, swollen rivers and gentle rains, dust-filled tempests and cooling zephyrs. In spring there were myriads of flowers and in autumn long, perfect days, gray and red and gold with the frost-bitten foliage of sage and scrub-oak and cottonwood, to dull the memory of that which had gone before and with certainty would follow after. In those wild and tempestuous surroundings were enacted the closing scenes of a mighty drama in which the first American made his last stand against the inevitable approach of civilization.

[3] Geologist W. E. Wrather suggested to the author that, as the climatic cycle moves in approximate periods of eleven, twenty-two, and forty-five years, the buffalo hunters and first cattlemen probably reached the Panhandle at the end of a long wet era (author's interview with W. E. Wrather; the transcript has been lost).

In the words of Stephen F. Austin, "Man rises from his primitive state as by the steps of a ladder. These are the laws of Nature, at times retarded and slow in operation, but certain in their results." Notwithstanding the fact that the Panhandle was a land of promise whose discovery was made as early as 1541, the latter half of the nineteenth century found it still a virgin country where buffalo grazed in countless herds and wild Indians pursued them undisturbed. It was not until the decade after the Civil War that there were set in motion the forces which cleared the plains and enlightened the world as to their potentialities.

In the late 1860's a stockman in the lower part of the state sought to turn his surplus cattle into much-needed cash by moving them overland from South Texas to a market in Kansas. With his long drive up the trail north, although he did not cross the Panhandle at the time, he set the precedent for a practice that led to the discovery of the fertility of a land heretofore considered a part of the Great American Desert.

While this was happening, hunters from Kansas were pushing down into the Cimarron region, the vanguard of the hordes destined to annihilate the buffalo and, without conscious effort, to exterminate the Indian by destroying his chief source of subsistence. After the hunter came the soldier to make safe through organized force the advance of civilization. Under his protection came the cowman to occupy the free range; close upon the heels of his success followed the merchant and farmer. With the advent of the latter appeared barbed wire and the railroad, and the frontier was no more.

During the time in which the plains emerged into prominence there arose on them five settlements whose names—Adobe Walls, Mobeetie, Tascosa, Clarendon, and Amarillo—will always be inseparably linked with any memory of the old West, because the characteristic quality of each was a typical expression of the distinct part played by some definite phase of the land's progress. The first of the settlements to come into existence was the trading-post called Adobe Walls, only a rude stockade erected on the Canadian River by a few hunters and merchants for safety and convenience, but destined to be the scene of an epoch-making fight between twenty-eight white men and several hundred Comanches, a fight that broke the morale of the Indian and brought the United States Army to protect the Panhandle.

A year later, in order to secure the peace achieved through military means, a post was established to the east on Sweetwater Creek. Soon the scattered occupants of the surrounding country moved in to live near an organized garrison and with their coming formed the nucleus of the first permanent settlement. There, under the shadow of the flag, the little town of Mobeetie, for so it was called at the last, became as it grew "the West's symbol of law and order. It was the first county seat and, as such, the governmental center of the twenty-six other counties attached to Wheeler County for judicial purposes. It held sway over an area of approximately fourteen thousand square miles and nine million acres of land."[4] Out from there, such men as Temple Houston, J. N. Browning, W. H. Grigsby, and Frank Willis journeyed "by buckboard to interpret and apply the law of the West in its and their own peculiar way."[5]

Farther to the west and north of the open range was Tascosa, founded by Spaniards and a soldier who had campaigned against the Indians. It was the wildest town on the frontier, where dark-skinned sheepherders from New Mexico and hard-drinking, straight-shooting cowboys thronged the streets; where Billy the Kid and his men traded; where the town's best gambler was a smiling Irishman who was followed everywhere by a pack of thoroughbred hounds. The girl who loved him was, so they say, a monte-dealing beauty from a dance hall in New Orleans.

Below the cap rock, on the "flat" where Carroll Creek joins Salt Fork, was the town of Clarendon, scoffingly called "Saints' Roost" because it was founded by a minister for the purpose of bringing religion and temperance to the frontier. With the increase in settlement it became the center of conflict between stockman and farmer as they struggled for possession of the land. Although most of its colonists eventually owned cattle, their primary motive was not to exploit an unpossessed territory for temporary advantage but to "take it up" legally and for permanence. With their coming began the slow but certain absorption of the range that continued till free grass was no more and its cattle barons were doomed to follow their predecessors, the buffalo and Indian, through the gates of history.

Nine years after the establishment of Clarendon the first railroad reached the Panhandle. As the tracks of the Fort Worth and Denver drew near from one direction and the Southern Kansas from another, a shrewd fellow named Berry predicted that wherever the two roads crossed, there would be the "queen city of the plains." His prophecy proved correct. Today, after many years, the metropolis of Northwest Texas is Amarillo, the outgrowth of Berry's townsite, Oneida. The original location has been moved

---

[4] L. F. Sheffy, "Old Mobeetie—The Capital of the Panhandle," *West Texas Historical Association Yearbook* 6 (1930), 5.

[5] Ibid., p. 14.

and the original name changed, but the city continues to grow and to fulfill in every way the ambition of the far-sighted man who conceived it.

As era followed era in rapid succession, each in passing left imprinted on the generations to follow the characteristics of the men bred by its specific needs. The first pioneers were reckless, roving adventurers who sought the frontier as much for the challenge it offered as for any material advantage. In direct contrast to these trailblazers were the settlers who followed after them, sober, industrious homeseekers, more often than not men of education and breeding. From the coalescence of these opposed types, their backgrounds and motives, evolved the tradition of the West of today with its crystallization in the person of that romantic figure, the cowboy, and its story, the story of the industry of which he and cattle and "free grass" formed the foundation.

To make comprehensible so rapid and complete a metamorphosis it is necessary to go back far enough into the history of the nation and the state to recount those factors which retarded for over three centuries the settlement of a region revealed to the white man during the first fifty years after Columbus's discovery of America, factors dealing with the nature of the area's original occupants and with the colonial policies of the two empires largely responsible for the early conquest of the North American continent.

As the French explorers for the most part were poor and few in number and through the character of their basic industry, the fur trade, were lured chiefly into well-watered and wooded regions, their influence in Texas was appreciable only as the motivating force behind the Spaniards. In the absence of more material attractions, the latter first expanded beyond the Rio Grande through fear of enemy encroachment in the direction of their rich and well-established state to the south.

When Cortez and his followers sailed from Spain, it was in quest of gold. Having arrived on the shores of Mexico, they found awaiting them a region perfectly suited to their purpose. There were precious metals beneath a fertile soil and a docile race possible of conquest and conversion to the Catholic faith.

But such was not the fortune of Coronado in the region now known as Texas. His "city of gold" proved to be a myth and the land around it a semi-arid expanse of prairie and plain inhabited by a primitive people who slept in tepees made of skins, lived on berries and wild game, possessed only articles easy to transport by dog travois, practiced no agriculture, and moved from place to place at will in pursuit of the buffalo. During his weeks of travel over and back across the plains, the Spaniard noted the terrain with accuracy, and, having arrived at the conclusion that it constituted an area unfit for the usages of civilized man, he dismissed it from his calculations and passed on to place his New Mexico among the more hospitable valleys of the upper Rio Grande.

In the preserved records of that journey originated the idea of the Great American Desert. So well was this fiction fostered by later explorers that by the beginning of the nineteenth century it had become a fact in the minds of the American public and its politicians. As a result, when, for the security and comfort of the advancing frontier, it seemed necessary to remove the southern semi-civilized Indians, the nation generally allotted to these tribes the distant plains area which, it was thought, lay too far beyond the Mississippi Valley to be reached at any time by the path of progress and even so would never be of any value to the builders of an agrarian civilization. In 1830 the law re-deeded to the rightful owners of the land that portion of the central plateau which lay between the Red River and the Platte.

But, contrary to expectation, by the middle of the century settlement had already extended to the edge of the Great Plains and was clamoring for an outlet to the frontier lying on the other side. The era of extensive land grants and railroad building followed, and in every plan for a Pacific line was the determination to clear the country of Indians for miles on either side of the proposed roadbed. The appropriation of the Indian Territory was the inevitable result.

Once again the original Americans were pushed aside, to the north and to the south, in order that a wide central tract might be left unobstructed as a passage across the continent from east to west. Soon population pressure brought about the organization of the northern portion into territories; only the southernmost reserve remained in the possession of the Indians, an area which, unfortunately for the Panhandle of Texas, adjoined it on its entire eastern side and by its proximity cut it off "from those natural routes of communication which otherwise would have been established with the Mississippi valley states."[6]

Long before the defining of a reserve, the Atlantic seaboard Indians had begun more or less voluntarily to withdraw westward in advance of the settlers and in turn forced before them the natives already inhabiting districts upon which they encroached. When, at last, the tribes dislocated by the white man had reached the edge of the

[6] B. B. Paddock, ed., *A Twentieth Century History and Biographical Record of North and West Texas*, I, 176.

woodlands, it was the Sioux who were forced out from their accustomed shade into the unfamiliar glare of the open plains where dwelled the wild Comanche.

Thus, with the newcomers' encroachment upon their native homeland began the steady southward migration that by the beginning of the eighteenth century placed the Comanches below the Arkansas River. There the Kiowa found them as they, too, moved down from the north, a bloody barrier which, being unable to remove, they were forced to become a part of.

About 1830 the Cheyennes and their Algonquian associates appeared in great numbers from beyond the Missouri to complete the savage confederacy which played so important a part in the history of Northwest Texas. Sometimes together, sometimes apart, the three tribes roamed back and forth over a range extending from the headwaters of the Red River to those of the Arkansas, and across Colorado, Texas, and Oklahoma, become one formidable, harmonious body through a common foe, the white hunter, and a common friend, the buffalo.

At the time of the discovery of America the bison grazed from the south of Texas to the Great Slave Lake in the north and from the prairies of the Mississippi Valley as far west as Idaho, Utah, and New Mexico. But his true home was the plains, and it was only after the settlements

approached the grasslands that he assumed importance in history.

From the first, the bison was the prey of the white man who pursued him so assiduously through all seasons of the year that by the beginning of the nineteenth century he was no longer to be found anywhere east of the Mississippi River. The construction of the Union Pacific and Kansas Pacific railroads led to his disappearance from the central plains. After that, only the northern and southern herds were left, with the latter occupying the same territory as that frequented by the Cheyenne, Kiowa, and Comanche Indians.

> Bison, like their Indian brother, were a nomadic animal, wandering always from one place to the other in search of fresh pasturage and migrating at the approach of winter from the high plains to warmer localities in the south. The herds moved along under the leadership of one patriarchal old bull, with the sexes keeping together throughout the year. As is usual among gregarious animals, there was constant fighting among the bulls for the supremacy of their band, the old leaders being overthrown by younger and more vigorous aspirants, as soon as their strength began to wane. Thus the very best sires were continually selected by the law of battle, the rutting season which announced their approach from far-off.[7]

[7] *Encyclopedia Americana* (1928), IV, 21.

Every need of the Indians' savage life the buffalo supplied. He was the inspiration for most of their pagan rituals and the source of all food, clothing, medicine, and shelter. His robe covered their beds, his dressed hide made moccasins, leggins, and portable tepees so necessary to their nomadic way. Braided rawhide made lariats and lines, and his skin made kettles for boiling meat, bullboats in which to ford streams, and trunks for the squaws' gewgaws. His bones made tools and his hoofs the glue with which feathers were attached to arrows and headpieces.

To the Plains Indian, the extermination of the buffalo was a pronouncement of doom. The settled Indian had other means of subsistence, but he had none.[8] The coming of the settler meant both the destruction of the animal

[8] According to C. S. Johnston, professor of archaeology at West Texas State Teachers' College (now West Texas State University), Canyon, Texas: "The Great Plains were from the earliest times (as far back as we know) inhabited by non-agricultural hunter types of Indians. It is a combination of the hunter type plus the agricultural Pueblo culture that we find making up the Slab-house culture so characteristic of Texas and Oklahoma. These Indians, judging from their pottery, seem to have lived down to the year 1300 in small villages. They practiced hunting and corn growing but were not highly civilized. They were crushed out of existence before the coming of the whites by the more warlike nomadic tribes of the Plains. These, chiefly the

without which it was impossible for him to live and the occupation of the hunting grounds which were a final refuge for red man and beast alike. In a desperate effort not to be dispossessed of lands that he considered his by right of heritage, the once friendly Comanche turned relentless foe, becoming the scourge of the Anglo-American and the factor which at the last retarded progress in Northwest Texas for a quarter of a century.

During the days of the Republic various policies were pursued in an effort to effect a permanent peace and to free the people from a conflict which was consuming energies otherwise needed to develop the country, but without results. When after annexation it became the duty of the United States government to protect the frontier, a cordon of military posts was established along its extending edge; later a large area was set aside for use as agency territory. But wild Indians outside the reserve continued their depredations, and reprobates within broke forth to indulge in marauding expeditions and murder. Having found no effective means of domiciling the Indians within the state, in 1859 the federal authorities removed as many as possible of them to the National Reserve. Through the Medicine Lodge Treaty of 1867 most of the tribes still outside were persuaded to enter, even the obdurate Cheyenne and Kiowa, and all of the Comanche but one band—the wild and implacable Kwahari whose range was upon the Staked Plains of the Northwest.

Of the many units which together formed the loosely organized Comanche tribe, only five require mention in this narrative—the Penatekas or "Honey-eaters," who lived below the Red River and were most closely associated with the general history of the state; the Yamparikas or "Root-eaters," the important northern division with whom the United States government had most of its contacts; the Kwahari, the "Antelope-skinners" who challenged all intruders upon their range and looked with scorn upon the more civilized tribes; the Quohadi, who fought at Adobe Walls; and the Nokoni or Detsanayuka[9] into whose midst Quanah Parker was born.

Apache, moved in. They practiced no agriculture and made no pottery but depended for their subsistence upon hunting and warfare (it was the Plains tribe the Spaniards found). They lived in small, temporary villages in tents known as 'tipis'" (C. S. Johnston to author, August 16, 1935, Lewis Papers, Archives, Dallas Historical Society).

[9] A Comanche division named for one of its chiefs after his death (Nokoni). *Nokoni*, or *Detsanyuka*, as they were also called, may be translated "bad campers . . . or people who never take trouble to fix up a good camp because they never stay long enough in one place" (Rupert Norval Richardson, *The Comanche Barrier to South Plains Settlement*, p. 20).

At the time of Texas' fight for independence young Peta Nokoni was rising into prominence as one of the principal war chiefs of the Nokoni. A few days after the decisive battle of San Jacinto, in the spring of 1836, the Nokoni warriors raided Parkers Fort, a settlement near the present town of Navasota. Among the captives taken was nine-year-old Cynthia Ann Parker,[10] who, after reaching early womanhood, became the girl-wife of the distinguished chief and the mother of his equally distinguished son, Quanah Parker.

Upon the destruction of the Nokoni camp on Pease River in 1860, at which time a general Indian slaughter was accomplished and Cynthia Ann was recaptured by the rangers, Quanah was adopted into the Kwahari band. It was one of fate's ironies that the last organized stand of redskin against white should be led by the halfbreed son of a settler's daughter and the young warrior she loved.[11]

[10] The story of Cynthia Ann Parker's life with the Indians, of her relationship with Chief Nokoni, and of her son, Quanah Parker, has been told many times. Somewhat varied accounts may be found in Richardson, *Comanche Barrier to South Plains Settlement*, in James T. DeShields, *Cynthia Ann Parker: The Story of Her Capture*, and in Paul I. Wellman, "Cynthia Ann Parker," *Chronicles of Oklahoma* 12, no. 2 (June 1934), 164.

[11] Quanah Parker's band was the last to enter the reservation in southwestern Oklahoma.

As the white man steadily advanced, the bison as steadily receded at the rate of about fifteen miles a year, with the Indian always close behind, until both had reached the western frontier and were chiefly concentrated in that part of Texas whose wildness and remoteness from the railroad made it least accessible to the encroachments of civilization. Meanwhile Quanah Parker had matured into a man. Each year had added to his influence. By 1870 he was at the height of his youthful ascendancy, a figure of great power, not only in his band but in the entire Comanche tribe, the only hope of the last Indian and his friend the buffalo as, together, they watched the white hunter draw nearer to the Panhandle Plains.

As the opening scene of the story unfolds, visualize a spacious and fertile land lying in an isolated position in the north of the state of which it is only nominally a part. On the hills to the west are scattered the villages and flocks of the remnant of a Spanish conquest. Above, a narrow strip of land cuts off Kansas and Colorado; and to the east arise the ominous tents of a warlike nation. The landscape is beautiful. Small lakes, "round as plates," break the level of the plains, and the "prairies are rolling fields of green." Thick groves of trees cluster in the creek beds and sagebrush; chaparral and mesquite cover the ground in pristine confusion. Except for a few Spanish families along the Canadian the only inhabitants are lobo-wolves, coyotes, jack rabbits, antelope, and the Indians who from time to time emerge from the shelter of the canyons to raid and fight or to pursue the buffalo that graze around them in herds of unbelievable numbers.

CHAPTER 2

The Vanguard of Civilization

(The Buffalo Hunter)

UNLIKE the Indian, civilized man slaughtered the bison in a most profligate manner. Sometimes the hams were picked for market; sometimes the meat was stripped and hung high in the trees to cure into jerky, and the tallow rendered for shortening. But, at first, the slaughter was accomplished as a general rule solely to procure the robe the buffalo offered. However, upon the discovery that money was also to be made from the green skins, properly tanned, hunting ceased to be a profitable sport and became, instead, the foundation of an industry which, during the few years of its existence, assumed enormous proportions and achieved far-reaching results only slightly connected with its real aim.

In the fall of 1870, W. C. Lobenstein and the two buffalo hunters, Charlie Rath and Charlie Myers, who acted as his agents in the collection and delivery of pelts from the Indians and other white trappers, were doing an extensive fur-trading business with headquarters at Fort Leavenworth, Kansas. Sometime during the winter they received an order from abroad for five hundred buffalo hides, to be used, so the buyers said, for experimental purposes in connection with tanning.

Among those drafted into the service of procuring the required hides was J. Wright Mooar, who happened at the time to be cutting timber for the government along Smokey Hill River. Finding some fifty or more hides on his hands after supplying his quota, he decided to follow the example of the foreign firm and do some investigating on his own. He acted quickly, and long before Lobenstein had heard from abroad, Mooar's merchandise had reached his brother John in New York and had found a ready market.

By 1872, Dodge City, Kansas, the terminus of the Santa Fe Railroad and soon to become the greatest hide market in the world, was a bustling box-town of hotels, supply stores, "fancy houses," and saloons; Myers and Rath were prosperous merchants, and the Mooar brothers were well established in the business of killing buffalo for shipment to markets in the east.

It was the greatest animal slaughter in history. As the bison retreated, the hunters moved quickly forward in pursuit. By 1873, Wright Mooar, who was in charge of the hunting division of his firm, and his outfit had drifted far beyond their usual territory, across that neutral strip known as "No Man's Land" and as far as the headwaters of Palo Duro Creek.[1] After an extended trip of several months to explore the new region, they returned to Kansas to tell of the discovery of a hunting ground ideal beyond belief.

Dodge City was the only railroad point within reach of the new section. Prompted by Mooar's report, a group of merchants decided to establish a trading-post immediately at some point on the beckoning Texas frontier. As an inducement to hunters, Myers, the leader, offered to pay a liberal freight rate for any merchandise delivered by them to the newly proposed trading-post. Among others who joined the party were Billy Dixon, a youngster from West Virginia who later won a Congressional medal for bravery in a skirmish with the Indians, William "Bat" Masterson, a newspaperman in the making, and James Hanrahan, a hunter on a large scale.

By spring, all arrangements were complete, and the caravan was packed for departure. The Cimarron River, toward which they headed, was the boundary line. Beyond that even the government offered no protection. The men were on their way into the unknown and knew it, a handful of adventurers pitting their luck against that of the Indians who awaited their coming.

But the hunters were a hardy breed, self-reliant and without fear. Like the red man in whose footprints they followed, they were men of action rather than thought, wholly unconcerned with matters of the intellect or the spiritual rewards of peace and security. Like him they desired not to build an empire, only to roam without restraint "among the streams and green grasses of the prairies and plains where the winds blew free and no lodges arose to break the light of the sun."[2]

At first the little party moved slowly. The hunters were well in advance of the buffalo and, furthermore,

[1] At the treaty meeting of Medicine Lodge in 1867, land south of the Arkansas River had been granted to the Indians to deter depredations. Although Indians and whites alike later believed the treaty prohibited white buffalo hunters' crossing the river into Indian lands, no clause of the treaty so provides, and no verbal promise to that effect would have been binding in Texas, which was not represented at the meeting and which still retained its public lands (G. Derek West, "The Battle of Adobe Walls [1874]," *Panhandle-Plains Historical Review* 36 [1963], 3).

[2] After a speech by Ten Bear, the Yamparika.

The Vanguard of Civilization 15

haste was impossible with wagons so heavily loaded with supplies. After crossing the line into Texas at a place where Buffalo Springs is today, they struck the breaks at the head of Moore Creek and followed them down to the point where the stream joined the Canadian. All along the banks on either side of the river were scattered the camps of other recent arrivals.

Turning east the men traveled only a short distance before coming upon some adobe ruins. Who their forerunners had been no one knew, but Billy Dixon vaguely remembered having heard tales while in the army of a trading-post connected with Bent's Fort.[3] These crumbled walls answered the description perfectly and were doubtless all that remained of a wilderness settlement where, according to legend, in 1839 over a hundred men had lived and busied themselves with articles of trade between St. Louis and Old Mexico.[4]

The location seemed ideal, but upon the discovery of a better one a few miles farther on, the wagons later pulled up to the new site, to which they gave the name Adobe Walls in honor of the historic ruins they had just seen.[5]

Tales of the country were not exaggerated. It was very beautiful and a hunter's paradise. Behind the little open plain on which the caravan camped lay numerous small hills. A mile away ran the Canadian River. In the many cottonwoods on the banks of its tributary creeks wild turkey roosted by the hundreds, and over the surrounding range moved thousands of buffalo as they migrated back and forth with the changes of season.

Within a few days Rath and his partner, R. M. Wright, arrived with the merchandise required for the opening of a general store. All hands fell quickly to work. After some weeks the sod structure which accommodated both their store and Hanrahan's saloon was complete.

[3] Bent's Fort, established by Charles, Robert, George, and William Bent and Ceran St. Vrain on the Arkansas River where it emerges onto the Great Plains, was one of the chief centers of the fur trade. Kit Carson and his mountain men headquartered there (Stanley Vestal, *Mountain Men*, p. 141).

[4] After his brothers died, William Bent continued to operate the fort. Married to a Cheyenne woman, he was influential among the Indians. He established a number of subposts; about a hundred men were employed at posts along the Canadian

(Rupert Norval Richardson, *The Comanche Barrier to South Plains Settlement*, pp. 77–78).

[5] With few exceptions the material for the entire Adobe Walls story has been taken from the author's interview with Olive King Dixon, widow of Billy Dixon, Amarillo, Texas, July 27, 1935 (transcript in the Lewis Papers, Archives, Dallas Historical Society).

Thomas O'Keefe had set up a blacksmith shop in a hastily thrown together picket house, but the main building of the settlement, built of adobe and cottonwood logs hauled in from Reynolds Creek, required more time for completion. When finished, although this structure housed the largest supply store of the settlement, that of Myers, the party's leader, and his partner, Fred Leonard, it was called "the fort" because of the picket stockade that encircled it and the thickness of the walls behind which were hidden extra guns and ammunition.

As soon as their presence was no longer needed, Dixon and the other hunters loaded their wagons and moved across the river to locate suitable camps on the south side. Having unpacked and "dug in," they settled down to await the coming of the buffalo. The hunters were not delayed long. Soon, with a low and unmistakable rumble, the first herd announced its approach. From then on there were long, busy days for all.

Some weeks later, Dixon found it necessary to go back to the settlement. A man named Bond, who had been working for him temporarily, accompanied him. At the river they were joined by another couple of hunters, from whom they heard the first account of a brutal massacre that had taken place at a nearby camp the day before. This was in June, 1874. On the morning following their arrival at Adobe Walls word reached them of another killing on Chicken Creek. With Indians on the warpath it would be impossible to continue the occupancy of isolated camps several miles from the protection of the fort. Their present mode of living had to be abandoned, for the time being anyway.

This much the hunters realized, but of the more significant aspects of the situation they remained in complete ignorance. For a year or more the restrictions of the reservation, the encroachment of the white man on their hunting grounds, and the needless slaughter of the buffalo had been feeding the fury of the Indians' resentment. They were in the mood to fight but lacked both the necessary leadership and the immediate incentive needed to go on the warpath.

In only rare cases had the government used force in placing the Indians on a reservation. As a result, there were still wandering at will over the Panhandle Plains three tribes, the Comanches, the Kiowas, and the Cheyennes, with the addition of a few Arapahoes.

Among the Quohadi band of the Comanches were two influential younger men: one was Quanah Parker, the halfbreed chief, and the other was Isatai,[6] the medicine man, who supposedly possessed a close relationship with

[6] West, "The Battle of Adobe Walls," p. 9.

the Great Father and had supernatural powers. Among other claims, he said he was able to mix a concoction which, when applied to the body, made it bulletproof.

That same spring, a relative of Isatai's had lost his life at the hands of a white man. Soon afterward, the Quohadi band of the Comanches held a medicine dance, an unusual proceeding for them. The Cheyennes and the Kiowas were invited to attend. At the end of the festival, the Comanches held a war council under the influence of the persuasive Quanah Parker and the vengeful Isatai. A concerted plan of action was agreed upon. The recent massacres were not, as the hunters had supposed, unrelated incidents, but the forerunners of a well-planned major attack.

News of the killings spread rapidly and by nightfall of the second day Adobe Walls was crowded with hunters who had hastily abandoned their outlying camps to seek shelter near the stockade. Luckily, a large supply of guns and ammunition had recently been hauled in. So starved, however, were most of the men for companionship that after the first excitement had passed, all danger from without was quickly forgotten in the pleasure of greeting and conversing with kindred spirits. Tales of adventures were exchanged; plans were made for the approaching days of affluence of which all seemed assured; fiddles whined forth, and with dancing and singing and not a premonition for the morrow, the little company made merry.

In the course of the evening, Dixon, after conferring with Hanrahan, decided to move the next day from his location some miles away and, having entered into partnership with the saloonkeeper, to set up camp closer to Adobe Walls. As he was most anxious to be off to an early morning start, he made his bed that last night in the open space near the blacksmith shop, staking his saddle pony nearby.

About two o'clock a noise like the discharge of a rifle aroused two men who were sleeping in the saloon. On investigation, the trouble proved to be only a cracking ridgepole, but, as the pole was the main support of the dirt roof, it had to be repaired at once to prevent the general collapse of the roof. Dixon and one or two others were sent to the creek to gather fresh timbers, a task which consumed the greater part of the night.

By the time they returned and their labor was finished, day was breaking and Dixon began at once to make preparations for leaving. Having rolled up his bed and thrown it on his wagon, he turned to untie his horse. To his surprise he found the horse nervously backing and pulling at the stake to which he was tethered. This fractious state in a usually docile animal caused Dixon to hesitate, knowing as he did that the pony, like many trained on the frontier, possessed the faculty of detecting from even a considerable distance the scent of the enemy it so greatly feared.

It was customary at the settlement to turn the stock out in the open valley to graze overnight. Looking in that direction, Dixon was able, with difficulty, to discern in the faint light a mass of figures apparently moving slowly toward the fort through the underbrush—probably, he first thought, the horses being driven in by the boy Oggs, whose job it was to round them up each morning. But on closer observation, the number appeared too large for that, and instantly his suspicions were aroused. He looked again, more intently, suspecting that the forms in the grass were Indians. For some unaccountable reason, his only thought was that they had slipped in to drive away the stock, a loss which would be disastrous to all concerned.

Quick action on his part was necessary. There was no time to arouse the other men, most of whom had settled down to sleep again after their return from the trip to the river. Dixon, an excellent shot, was confident anyway that one or two well-aimed loads, even at that distance, would create havoc among the marauders and cause them to relinquish their booty and flee. His own pony by this time was in such a state of terror that its frantic lunging threatened momentarily to uproot its stake from the ground, so he stopped long enough to retie it to his wagon before raising his gun to take aim.

In the short interval the light of day had increased enough for him to distinguish with ease objects which a few minutes before had been scarcely perceptible. The sight that met his eyes was far from the expected one. There were no riderless horses and no circling Indians. Instead, in the orderly manner of a trained battalion, the enemy moved slowly forward, several hundred strong.

Evidently the attack had been planned for many weeks, with scouts reconnoitering after dark until perfectly familiar with the fort and the camps immediately surrounding it. Every move of Dixon's had been observed from the first. When he raised his gun, the Indians knew that they were detected and that stealth was no longer an advantage. A bugle sounded, and with a savage warwhoop they put their horses to a run and advanced like the wind.

The Comanches were the finest horsemen ever on the plains and rode ponies so perfectly trained that not only could they be stopped within their own length while going at full speed, but they could be turned completely around without the use of reins, thus leaving the warrior's arms free to handle any weapon—arrow, tomahawk, or gun.

Suddenly there were Indians on all sides; naked

bodies and animal flanks alike shone with black war paint and fantastic designs in yellow, ochre, and green. Bells jingled from the ponies' bridles and red flannel waved from their plaited tails. And at the head of the yelling band came Quanah Parker, fierce eyes gleaming and on his head the bonnet of the occasion, a trailing head-piece of eagle feathers that reached to his horse's hoofs. Straight up to the fort they rode, through the picket stockade, wheeling their mounts to kick at the doors.

The hunters had been sleeping scattered around in the open stockade and in the shops. The war-whoop and the bugle aroused them. Despite the abrupt awakening, their confusion was of only a few seconds' duration. They were all real frontiersmen, absolutely without fear, cool of head, and quick to act in time of stress. Also, most of them were hunters who not only shot well but went always armed with deadly long-distance rifles.[7] Those outside the main building made quickly for the interior of the fort. Hanrahan assumed command at once. With great haste, large bags of flour, meal, and corn, of which there was an abundance, were piled against the walls as barricades, after which the men quickly took their places at improvised port-holes, large enough to assure a view of the enemy and with room for a gun.

The only persons left to the savagery of the Indians were two freighters who had driven in the night before with a load of supplies. Taken unawares as they slept in their wagon, they were quickly shot and scalped, as was their pet Newfoundland dog, whose body was later found lying beside them with a memento of hide neatly cut from his back.

One of the youngest hunters, Billy Tyler, upon venturing into the open, was struck at the beginning of the fight. Spurred on by the loss of a comrade, the besieged men made every shot count. Full daylight revealed dead Indians everywhere. Indians disliked losing their warriors and preferred retreat to victory earned at too great a cost. Little by little, as the long-range rifles continued a deadly fire, they began to fall back to regroup their forces for a fresh attack. Assault after assault was made without success. Among the casualties were two Cheyennes, Horse Chief and the son of Chief Stone Calf.[8] Quanah Parker's horse was shot from under him, but he managed to crawl to safety. He was slightly wounded by a ricocheting bullet

[7] "By 1870 the Sharps Rifle Company had converted large numbers of their breech-loading percussion models to take fixed ammunition. At the same time they began the production of a new series of heavy, single-shot, breech-loading rifles, with calibres ranging from .45 to .50, specially designed for killing big game" (West, "Battle of Adobe Walls," p. 2).

[8] Ibid., p. 20.

and was forced to lie in wait until a comrade picked him up. During all the fighting Isatai had occupied an observation post far beyond bullet range.

By early afternoon the attacks had stopped and the Indians had withdrawn to confer among themselves. However, whenever an emissary attempted to move with a message from one group to another, he was quickly picked off by a shot from the fort. By late afternoon the Indians had come to a full realization that Isatai was a false prophet and that the hunters were not going to give up the fort. One by one they mounted their ponies and slowly rode away.

The besieged men were not surprised at the withdrawal, for they were familiar with the fact that the Indians never fought unless they felt they had a decided advantage and with the Indian superstition that a warrior whose body was not recovered or whose scalp had been taken could not enter "the happy hunting ground."

As soon as the Indians had retreated into the distance, a few of the settlers stepped forth to check up and to bury the dead. Others hastened to reinforce the stockade against a much-dreaded second attack and to construct on top of the fort a look-out where a constant watch might be kept.

But the Indians did not return. During the following few days several parties of two or three were seen in the distance, but no further attack was made. As the news spread, men from everywhere flocked to the fort until there were over two hundred crowded there, all clamoring for an immediate return to Dodge City. However, there were obstacles other than savages to overcome before that could be accomplished. Not a horse or team of oxen remained after the raid. Those few brought in by late arrivals were not adequate for all. Besides, the first thing of importance was to get word to the federal authorities in Kansas. After hours of serious conference, Henry Lease volunteered to go for assistance, riding alone over one hundred and eighty miles of trail, through a country alive with Indians bent on massacre. Despite the numerous perils which confronted him, he arrived safely in Dodge City, and the message was quickly forwarded to Fort Leavenworth, the most important post near the North Texas frontier.

CHAPTER 3

The Soldier

DURING the period preceding and including the years 1870–1874, the regular army had been involved to some extent in the warfare on the western front, which included the Panhandle. But it was not until after the episode at Adobe Walls that the War Department resolved either to subjugate without compromise or to annihilate the three wild tribes still roaming outside the reservations.

By late summer a two-part campaign had been organized. Three commands were ordered into the field by General John Pope, commanding general of the Department of the Missouri, one of them being that of Colonel Nelson A. Miles from Fort Dodge, Kansas. At the same time General C. C. Augur, commander of the Department of Texas, had ordered the formation of three columns: one under Colonel John Davidson, operating west from Fort Sill; one under Lieutenant Colonel George P. Buell, operating east from New Mexico; and one under Colonel Ranald S. Mackenzie, well seasoned by previous experience with the Comanches, operating north from Fort Concho.[1] The plan was to converge on the Panhandle with Miles moving south from Kansas. Each command would include several companies of cavalry, a complement of infantry, a supply train with provisions for six weeks, and thirty to forty scouts.

From the beginning to the end of the campaign, the life of the soldiers was hard. The particular "hostiles" they were pursuing had long since entrenched themselves in an area that provided two powerful topographic lines of defense: one the great belt of gypsum or "bad water" country that crossed the plains from north to south; the other, the foothill slopes of the rugged cap rock escarpment. The soldiers, being unfamiliar with both the nature of the terrain and the great extremes of climate, were unprepared to cope with the conditions that surrounded them. The thermometer at times reached 110 in the shade. For the thirst aroused by such extreme heat, often the only water obtainable lay in buffalo wallows, holes that were hot, stagnant, foul-smelling, and covered with slime. The supply trains were often unable to keep in close contact with the troops and, being far to the rear, were subject to frequent attacks and loss. Camp was broken each morning at

[1] William H. Leckie, "The Red River War, 1874–1875," *Panhandle-Plains Historical Review* 29 (1956), 83–85.

five in order to accomplish, in spite of such adverse conditions, a daily march of some twenty-five miles. There were occasional skirmishes with the Indians, and much harassment at night by Indian attempts to drive off the horses.

Miles was well into Texas by the latter part of August. On August 30, 1874, he had a stiff encounter with the Cheyennes on a small plain close to the north fork of the Red River. On the morning of September 9, he and his train were again attacked as they approached the ridge between the Canadian and the Washita rivers. This battle continued for two or more days and left many wounded and several dead. Buell and Davidson also met face to face with the enemy on various occasions, but it was not until Mackenzie's victory at the Palo Duro that the Indians' resistance began to falter and their spirit to break. By late August, Mackenzie and his column had reached Fort Concho.[2]

On August 23, his command, with a greatly increased force, left Fort Concho for the High Plains. In preparation for the campaign, he had formed a new scouting party composed of six white men, thirteen Seminoles, twelve Tonkaway Indians, and a few Lipans. Lieutenant William A. Thompson was placed in charge. After about ten days, the command arrived in the region of Catfish Creek, not far from the mouth of Cañon Blanco. They remained in this vicinity for about two weeks to rest the men, to get additional supplies, and to reconnoiter.

On September 19, the command was joined by Mackenzie and additional troops. On the following morning they broke camp to march in the direction of the Palo Duro. The plan was for Davidson to take up a position on Otter Creek and for Buell to range between him and Mackenzie. The days that followed were unbelievably difficult. There was a severe electrical storm followed by a downpour of rain. It required twelve mules to pull a single supply wagon to the base of the steep incline to the plains. Often the cavalry troops were forced to walk rather than ride through the mud. The mules were unable to get the supply train to the top, and it was only by the combined efforts of pulling and pushing mules and men that the feat was accomplished. They reached the High Plains September 25. Without waiting for the slower moving supply train and infantry, the cavalry pushed on twelve miles farther to Tule Spring, which was to be their temporary base of action. After dark they moved out to investigate their surroundings, and, on finding no Indians, spent the night and the following day in a ravine. About five o'clock in the afternoon they moved on to a not-too-distant freshwater lake and made camp.

[2] R. G. Carter, *On the Border with Mackenzie*, p. 474.

At about ten-thirty that night a large party of Indians attacked in an attempt to run off the horses. The effort was futile, for Mackenzie had given strict orders that all the horses be staked and hobbled. Several hours later the Indians retired to a distant position from which they continued firing toward the camp all night.

At five-thirty in the morning of the twenty-seventh, they attacked again, but the attack was of short duration. Very quickly they were in flight, with Captain Boehm and Captain Gunther and their troops in pursuit. They followed the Indians for only a few hours, then returned to the lake camp for breakfast and to report to Mackenzie that the Indians were following a course to the east. Probably because of scouting reports of an encampment in Palo Duro, Mackenzie assumed that the hostiles had taken this particular direction in order to create confusion as to the location of their encampment. He forbade further pursuit and rested his command quietly until three in the afternoon, when he ordered the cavalry to remount. For twelve hours they rode in a northwesterly direction, and then stopped to catch much-needed sleep. Very shortly, at four o'clock, they were up again and mounted. It was still dark when they resumed their march, still going north. As daylight broke there came into view for the first time the long, wide, multicolored chasm known as the Palo Duro Canyon. Rocky walls arose straight up on either side to a distance of five or six hundred feet in some places. Through the center of the basin, the Ceta Creek proceeded on its way to join the Prairie Dog Fork of the Red River. On either side of the creek were various lodges composed of innumerable tepees. It was evident from the size that the encampment included Kiowas and Cheyennes, as well as Comanches. It was a serene domestic scene. Buffalo skins lay all around, drying in the sun, and ponies grazed peacefully everywhere.

It required some time to find a path into the canyon. Captain Beaumont and his troop were the first to enter. The way down was rugged and perilous, and it became necessary for each rider to dismount and lead his horse in single file. At sight of the first soldier, an Indian sentinel fired his gun and waved a red blanket. Hundreds of Indians poured from the tepees, stopping only long enough to untie their horses before fleeing toward the mouth of the canyon several miles distant. A few of the braver warriors scurried up the walls to take a protected position behind the boulders.

Captain Beaumont's troop was quickly followed by two other troops under the leadership of Mackenzie himself. When they reached the basin, Mackenzie ordered the men to pursue the fleeing Indians down the canyon. Very quickly the Indians on the canyon walls opened fire, but luckily for the soldiers, only one man was wounded.

During the same period, Captain Beaumont and his men had been busy rounding up the ponies and driving them back toward the advancing soldiers. Seeing that there was to be no fight, Mackenzie ordered his men to dismount quickly and proceed with the real business of the day, which was to destroy the encampment. As soon as the tepees were torn down and the poles that held them were broken to bits, and the vast quantities of flour, sugar, and dried buffalo meat that had been stored for winter had been made inedible, he gave orders to return to the plains.

Once on top they were joined by the troops they had left behind as a protection for their safe exit. The command quickly fell into a formation of columns with the ponies well guarded in the center. Within a short time, they were ready to start the march back to Tule Spring. The following morning, at Tule Spring, the Indian scouts were allowed to select for their own personal use the finest of the Indian ponies, and the remainder were shot to prevent their recapture by the Indians.

The idea of the campaign was never to conquer by a single decisive victory but to bring the Indians to surrender through the continued harassment of being driven from one fastness to another. On they went with the troops close upon their heels, retreating through the breaks, across the canyon, and out between its protecting walls to the desolate ground on top.

By late fall, many of their villages were burned, their ponies killed, their supplies captured and destroyed, and they themselves were wandering on foot over the High Plains in sleet and snow. The winter that followed proved their final undoing. One by one, family by family, group by group, they turned toward the reservation. There was no alternative. By June, 1875, not one remained outside.[3] The army stood supreme; the day of the Indians was no more. Bewildered and humbled, he who once had been prince of the plains made ready for his last march—down the white man's trail to civilization and obscurity.

After annexation, when the United States govern-

---

[3] Quanah Parker remained an influential leader after his people settled on reservation lands. Convinced that the Indian could survive only through education and adapting to the white man's ways, he did much to civilize those under his leadership. His proposal to lease surplus reservation pasture land substantially increased the annual income of his people. He served as judge of the Indian Court and as his tribe's emissary to Washington and was the first to sign the treaty opening reservation lands to settlers ("Quanah Parker," *Encyclodepia Americana* [1928], XXIII, 56–57).

ment assumed from the Republic the responsibility of protecting the Texas frontier, its first move, as has already been stated, was to establish a cordon of military posts, the purpose of which was not only to clear the way for the oncoming settler, but also to make permanent his safety after arrival. In pursuance of this policy, at the conclusion of the campaign, immediate steps were taken by the War Department for placing a post in the Panhandle region.

Major Biddle was ordered to assume command on Miles's return to Kansas and to commence, as soon as possible, the construction of barracks large enough to accommodate four or five hundred men. Shortly "a long caravan of wagons, loaded with lumber and supplies, and drawn by oxen and mule teams, was wending its way down the trail from Dodge City, its destination being Hidetown on Sweetwater Creek."[4]

By June 5, 1875, there had arisen on the slope of the creek, like a "sentinel of civilization," the fully organized military post of Fort Elliott, first known as the "Cantonment of Sweetwater" but later named in honor of Major Joel H. Elliott of the Seventh Cavalry, who had been killed in a battle of that regiment with the Indians on the

Washita River, Indian Territory, November 27, 1868, at the time Black Kettle's village was destroyed.

Sweetwater Creek had been discovered twenty-five years before, and, because of the excellent quality of its water, so named by Captain McClellan, as he and his party scouted over the country in the first organized exploring trip into the Red River region. The land was made a military reservation through the purchase by the government of 2,600 acres from William Walter Phelps. Long, rambling frame and adobe structures, like huge barns, were built in a rectangular formation, in the center of which were the parade grounds. The offices were in front; on one side were the sleeping quarters of the enlisted men with their dining rooms and kitchens adjoining at the back. On the opposite side were the quarters of the officers and their families.

In the extreme rear were the houses of the black families, and down on the creek the tepees of friendly Indians, who had either been sent from the reservation or acquired during the summer's campaign—a necessary addition to the personnel of any frontier army because of their knowledge of the country and the wiles and crafts of their own people. The black troops, of which there were almost as many as white, were from Fort Concho at San Angelo. Added to these were the white soldiers, men of every sort

[4] L. F. Sheffy, "Old Mobeetie—The Capital of the Panhandle," *West Texas Historical Association Yearbook* 6 (1930), 3.

from everywhere, an altogether heterogeneous group, welded into a working unit only by the intelligence and tact of the men in command.

The Indians camped with their families by the water's edge, living under conditions as free as possible from restrictions, considering the necessary regulations of army life. An interpreter and his wife, Indian Fanny, acted as their spokesmen. They were privileged to retain their language and primitive customs, except in rare instances when, for reasons of order or sanitation, some ritual was forbidden—such as placing the dead, wrapped in the gaudiest of calicoes, high in the treetops in a swing made of woven boughs, for the vultures to destroy.

On the whole they were peaceful and contentedly subservient to the white man's orders, giving trouble only when they came into the possession of liquor. When drunk, they went wild and invariably resurrected their feathers, paint, and tomahawks, and attempted to go on the warpath. The officers were understanding men and treated such outbursts, even though they sometimes resulted in murder, as misdemeanors, punishable as such by a night in the guardhouse or by some other means equally lenient. For the purveyor of the strictly forbidden "firewater," whoever he might be, it was an entirely different matter. This culprit, if apprehended, never failed to receive a term of several years in the federal penitentiary as a punishment for interference with the wards of the government.

Married black soldiers were allowed to remain at night with their families, who lived in separate houses behind the barracks. These families, when the troops moved from post to post, moved with them, traveling a few miles to the rear of the infantry in great army wagons drawn by four spans of mules and overflowing with household goods, out of which at the most unexpected places peeked the black faces of innumerable children. When they stopped to make camp, the women did their cooking, and the rations supplied them were the same as the soldiers'. At night the animals were held in rope corrals while the teamsters stood guard. In case of danger, the drivers were reinforced by a detachment of soldiers.

When they were settled, the wives did laundry work or other small tasks around the post to make extra change. The men enjoyed the same privileges as the white recruits and were elevated to the position of petty officer when merit warranted a reward. There were schools for the children where the three races sometimes studied together, but more often the little Indians and Negroes were segregated and taught by both black and white instructors, under the general supervision of a white officer.

The officers and their families held themselves quite aloof, not only from the enlisted men, but from the neighboring townspeople as well, appearing outside the army grounds only when, as single men, they chose to amuse themselves at the dance halls, saloons, and gambling resorts on "the hill," or, as married men, rode forth in state on fancy saddle horses, accompanied by wives who sat gracefully in side saddles and wore flowing habits of black velvet and tiny hats trimmed in long plumes.

Among other pleasures, there were bands to parade by, orchestras to dance to, ambulances in which to ride with one's best girl. There were excellent physicians and an infirmary equipped with the most modern conveniences. There was much social activity and little work of a serious nature, as the military maneuvers were concerned chiefly with the occasional pursuit of some runaway from the reservation. The result made life at this one frontier post, at least, a most enjoyable affair.

Before the "Cantonment" was established near Sweetwater Creek, a small band of hunters chose for their operating base and freighting point the locality where the trail to Dodge City crossed the creek. Soon a storekeeper and saloon man established themselves for business amid the numerous wagons, tepees, and piles of skins that lay scattered around on the prairie, and by their addition converted a campground into a settlement which in time came to be called very appropriately "Hidetown."

But the presence of rowdy huntsmen and bullwhackers within the neighborhood of a garrison proved disastrous to discipline. Consequently, soon after the establishment of Fort Elliott, the military authorities forced their removal to a camp a mile or so away. However, as a result of an Indian scare, they were later allowed to return to a position close enough to be under protection of the soldiers.

The new site, with its enforced dignity, seemed to demand a more suitable name, and "Hidetown" was changed to Sweetwater, which, in turn, because of confusion with another town similarly designated, was changed to Mobeetie, the Comanche word of the same meaning. Upon the organization of Wheeler County in 1879, all the other Panhandle counties, including Greer, which is now in Oklahoma, were attached to Wheeler County for judicial purposes. Mobeetie was made the county seat, the first in the northwest, and, as such, grew into the "mother city which nurtured and molded a vast territory into other units as each in time came of age."[5]

[5] B. B. Paddock, ed., *A Twentieth Century History and Biographical Record of North and West Texas*, I, 159.

CHAPTER 4

The Peaceful Invasion

(The Longhorn and the Trail Driver)

AFTER the enforced withdrawal of the Indians from the Panhandle Plains, there was no further need for a garrison, so within a few years the frontier post of Fort Elliott was abandoned. Within these few years, hunters by the thousands invaded the region. The hunting was done in many ways, sometimes by families who lived the year round in covered wagons, following as the prey moved on, and sometimes by youngsters armed with revolvers and riding ponies trained in Indian fashion. But most often, the hunters operated in groups of three or more, living in temporary camps from which they hunted on horseback and on foot, with the aid only of plenty of ammunition and "resting sticks" upon which to support their cumbersome, eighteen-pound long-range rifles.[1] As the buffalo

disappeared, there loomed into view from the south another quadruped—slender, long legged, fast of movement, narrow faced, shabby, nervous, and with huge horns, an animal destined to play an important part in the history, economy, and legends of the state—the Texas longhorn.

When the first Texans moved into the valley of the Colorado to settle, they found surrounding them a mounted population, the Mexican *rancheros* and the Plains Indians. Both practically lived on horseback. From their foes the Anglo-American colonists learned a new method of warfare out of which came the Texas ranger and the six-shooter, and from their Mexican neighbors a new method of stock raising, a method that changed cattle from a prosaic "incident in agriculture" to the basis of an industry and produced the most colorful figure in the pageant of America—the cowboy.

---

[1] The killing itself was not difficult, as the clumsy "brutes" they pursued were as timid as deer, none too quick of movement and a target of size impossible to miss. The procedure was to follow the tracks of the herd to a water hole, then lie in wait. The leader was killed first, after which the confusion of the other milling animals made a general slaughter easy, a highly lucrative but most unsporting method. Enough were killed at one time to require several days of skinning. In each camp there was usually one man elevated to the position of killer, while the others did the supposedly more menial work of dressing. The head was skinned first, then tied to a stake, after which the hide was ripped down the center and pulled off by ox teams. It was stretched on the ground for a few days to dry before being stacked for freighting (B. B. Paddock, ed., *A Twentieth Century History and Biographical Record of North and West Texas*, I, 113).

A difficult economic situation awaited the paroled Confederate soldier on his return home at the end of the Civil War. He had neither money nor a job but had accumulated taxes that had to be paid. However, in Texas there was one thing in abundance—cattle. Since the Mexicans' abandonment of their ranches during the days of the revolution, the *rancheros*' herds had roamed wild and multiplied at a prodigious rate. There they were—the potential fortune of any man who cared to make them his own by the simple process of placing his brand on them with a hot iron.

The only problem was marketing. Even though Texas later gained wide recognition economically as a cattle state, in the beginning there was insufficient demand for beef or hides within its own boundaries. The only markets at that time were in the more densely populated areas to the north, and the day of the railroad and easy transportation had not yet reached the Southwest. Although trail driving had been practiced for many years, it did not become common until after the war, when a combination of conditions made it the logical answer to a pressing need. Gradually, the taste for beef spread from the original consumers—the Indians and soldiers at the posts—to the American public in general, and the demand increased accordingly. On Christmas Day, 1865, the Union Stockyards were opened in Chicago. Two springs later, the tracks of the Kansas Pacific reached the last settlement in western Kansas, and an Illinois stock raiser, James McCoy, chose its temporary terminus as the point at which to build his cattle pens. Texas had an outlet at last.

When the practicality of trail driving became an established fact, there sprang into existence great overland arteries of commerce, the subsidiary vessels of which extended until the Panhandle was covered by a network of trails running in all directions. Over these frontier highways during a quarter of a century passed millions of cattle, and behind them rode the bearers of such revered names as Blocker, Fant, Glidden, Ellis, Howard, Ikard, Worsham, Blair, Belcher, Clerk, Eddlemans, and Dubose.

Centuries before the coming of the longhorn, long before Coronado crossed the Great Plains into New Mexico to blaze the way for the conquering white race, there lay scattered along the Canadian River many small villages of neat and substantial slab houses, the homes of the settled Pueblos who had drifted from the west to live among the Basket-Maker Indians of the Panhandle.

Little did they imagine, as they planted corn seed on the banks of the nearby stream or molded vessels from the white sands at their feet, that other peoples, as had they, were "to come, to see, and to conquer"—the warring

Apache close upon their own heels, then the Comanche as he followed the trail of the buffalo, traders to barter for stolen stock, Spanish sheepherders in search of pasture lands, and last, a young army blacksmith with his vision of a future white civilization.

It was during the years immediately preceding the blacksmith's coming that the first of the *pastores* drifted in from New Mexico to graze their flocks up and down the river for a distance of some fifty miles. Their camps were situated at various outlying locations, but their families, for purposes of safety and convenience, were congregated around a central square which, according to native custom, they termed a plaza, this particular one being known by the name of Barago or Juan Domingo.

Of the various countrymen of theirs who established like settlements within the next few years, only five will be mentioned: Charves, because of his success in promoting the largest plaza of all; Ortega, because it was near him the soldiers first camped; Trujillo, because his site was destined to become the headquarters of the LS Ranch; Ysibel Gurule, for no good reason other than the euphony of his name; and Casimero Romero, because of his wealth and influence generally.

It was the last mentioned who in 1874 moved from Anton Chico with his Castilian wife to live among the willows growing on an island at the mouth of the creek which became Tascosa Creek. Soon a long line of freight wagons was plying ceaselessly between Romero's new location and Las Vegas and Dodge City, and his home had become the center of all the cultural activities of the Mexican families living around him. In the long hall that extended the length of his large adobe house, the first fiestas were held and also those occasional masses for which Father De Marra journeyed from afar that he might baptize the newborn, marry the young, and partake of the Lord's Supper with the Catholic communicants on the surrounding frontier.

One day in 1874 a company of soldiers stopped on their way to the Palo Duro breaks to camp and rest overnight beneath the tall cottonwoods that grew near the Ortega Plaza. Their march had been long and dry and hot, and the picture formed by a shaded grove on the side of a swift and wide freshwater stream made so deep an impression on one of the party that he vowed at the expiration of his enlistment to come back and make the place his permanent home.

However, when Henry Kimball, for that was the soldier's name, did return, in 1876, it was not at this exact location that he unpacked his blacksmith tools, but across the *atascosas* (boggy islets) on the island upon which stood Romero's hacienda. There Charles Goodnight and his party discovered the soldier and his companion as the rancher passed on his way to place his first herd of cattle in the Palo Duro Canyon.

At about the same time, G. T. Howard from New Mexico and his German Jewish partner, Ira Rinehart, moved in to establish a store in which whiskey, drugs, patent medicine, and staples were to be sold. A year later James E. McMasters arrived, and he was quickly followed by other merchants—Armstrong, Willingham, and East. Before many years had passed, this small group had banded together to control the business affairs of the settlement, which by that time bore the official name of Atascosa.

When John Cone, a wealthy businessman, became attracted to the fast-developing region, he was unable to purchase within the established business district a location for his prospective store because of the unwillingness of the merchants to encourage competition. But Cone, who was not easily turned from his original purpose, finally succeeded in buying from Romero a tract large enough to accommodate the long adobe building required for his plans. Close by would be a corral large enough to accommodate the horses of visiting cowboys.

When the first mail routes were established in 1878, the little settlement dropped the opening "A" from its name to become officially known as Tascosa.

The following years were those of the range's most rapid development. Soon every acre of the public domain was under the legal or arbitrary control of some large cattle outfit. Upon the organization of Oldham County in 1880, the town became the county seat and, as such, was the focal point for all trade and for the settlement of all judicial matters pertaining to the interests of the industry upon the rise of which its growth was dependent. Mobeetie was, it is true, the capital of the Panhandle, but Tascosa was destined to become the capital of the "Kingdom of Free Grass."

Having entered the Union under conditions out of the ordinary, Texas, contrary to usual procedure, was allowed by the agreement of annexation to retain "all unappropriated lands, said lands to be applied to the payment of the debts and liabilities of the Republic and the residue thereafter to be disposed of as the state might direct."

As a result, the millions of acres of undeveloped region known as the public domain were immediately divided by legislation into various classes, among which were school and university lands, railroad grants, and veterans' grants, the revenue from the sale of the first to be used in the erection of institutions for public education, the second class to be offered as an inducement to the rail companies to build railroads across the uninhabited areas, and the last to be given in lieu of cash payment for services rendered during the Mexican wars. Sixteen railroad certificates, each certificate the equivalent of a section of land, were given as bonus for every mile of main track constructed. The soldiers' grants or veterans' certificates comprised a larger territory, each one being equal to several thousand acres.

As colonization was a necessary object in the progress of the state, the first important step was to have a survey made of the lands set aside for railroad and for school purposes. Although there were individual surveyors with small outfits who accomplished some of the work, the greater part of the surveying and locating of the Panhandle was made by the Sherman firm of Gunter, Munson and Summerfield. They received land certificates, or "scrip," in payment for their services.

The land was surveyed in what, for want of a better name, is called the "checkerboard" system; that is, for every railroad section surveyed and located, an adjacent section was simultaneously surveyed and numbered with a succeeding number, the one always even, the other odd. In this way, an effort, to a great extent unsuccessful, was made to keep the country open for settlement by prevent-ing the accumulation of large blocks by individuals or companies.

A few exceptions to this policy were made, such as deeding to each county a block of twenty or more sections for a county school fund, and the one or two more notable cases where huge reserves were set aside for the express purpose of financing some project necessary to the development of the country, such as the building of the state capitol at Austin.

Naturally, it was not land but money the railroads and surveying firms wanted. So much of the scrip as soon as acquired was put up for sale as low as thirty cents an acre or even one hundred dollars a section. In general the scrip was sold by stockbrokers, but in the Panhandle it was available direct from the railroad, surveying firms, or local representatives of either. Gunter, Munson and Summerfield were among the largest speculators in the field.

From the accounts of the many hunters, soldiers, and trail drivers who crossed the Panhandle during the first years after the fight at Adobe Walls, a new and true conception of the land arose and, as word spread to distant parts, it caused the region that heretofore had been considered without value except as a basis for speculation to become a focus of attention for financier and settler alike.

Suddenly, there began to flow in from all over the

Union and across the seas as well that tide of immigration which was to change the plains and prairies into one vast open range.

There was living in Colorado at this time one Charles Goodnight, a frontiersman to whom the whole of Texas was a familiar region. Although born in Illinois, he had been brought to the Southwest as a child and had spent many of his formative years in pursuits common to the new country. He had been at different times a farmer, a cowboy, a clerk, a trail driver, a ranger, and an army scout.

It was while serving with Norris's regiment during the Civil War that he crossed and recrossed the High Plains and, in passing, paused often to look down upon the well-watered and protected area that lay within the steep walls of the Palo Duro Canyon and to wonder if the land lying there would not make as ideal a cattle ranch as it was making a stronghold for the Comanches and their grazing ponies.

Later, after the panic of 1873, during which the earnings of years were wiped away, the scene reappeared before him with such force that he determined to forego the more or less settled life he had been living since his marriage and return to the fertile region of the grasslands to the south.

During this period, the financial headquarters of the world were in London, and most American ventures operated to a great extent on British capital and for British stockholders as well. Ranching appealed particularly to the gentry produced by the traditions of agrarian civilization. It was not only a pursuit with which they were congenial by nature but also one that, because of its connection with the land, was not closed to them through the edicts of an aristocracy that discouraged active participation in trade. As a result, upon the opening of the Northwest, there was a general influx of younger sons from England.

Among the many whom Goodnight knew was James Hughes, whose father was the author of *Tom Brown's School Days*. Although both men were more or less established in Colorado, their interest was focused on Texas. His one chance to recover his losses, Goodnight thought, was to reestablish himself in the land of his initial success. But insufficient capital prevented that. Hughes, for his part, had money in plenty but was handicapped through lack of practical knowledge. The needs of the two were mutual.

Sometime during the year of the failure of the bank in which Goodnight was so heavily involved, he trailed down into the Pecos country to receive and deliver a bunch of steers bought by a man named Snider from John

Chisum. In order to gain experience, Hughes went along as a member of the outfit. So well pleased was he with his introduction to the South Plains that immediately upon his return to Colorado he and another Britisher, named Johnson, also eager to operate in Texas, bought a third interest, each, in the herd that Goodnight was ranging eight miles beyond Pueblo on the south bank of the Arkansas.

These cattle, simply good, plain, colored cows,[2] heifers, and Kentucky bulls, were the first of the herd of sixteen hundred which a winter or so later were pointed in the direction of the scattered lakes and succulent grasses of the Llano Estacado. Besides the three owners, the outfit included Goodnight's brothers-in-law, the Dyer boys—Walter, Sam, and Leigh—two Mexicans, a cook, and a trail boss, Dave McCormick, who had been in the employ of Goodnight for several years. The party moved slowly as the cattle grazed and drifted along, first toward the Cimarron, then on to the Canadian and across into New Mexico, where they stopped for the winter. After estab-

2 "When the wild cattle (from the rancheros) 'black with brown backs and bellies' in time became mixed with the domestic cattle, their calves took on mixed colors" (J. Frank Dobie, *The Longhorns*, p. 20). "There was always a leader, who assumed his place at the head of the herd and there kept it day after day, behind him the color-spotted ribbon that stretched out from a quarter of a mile to two miles or more" (ibid., p. 71).

lishing camp, Goodnight returned to Colorado for a few months.

When he rejoined the outfit in the spring, he found that during his absence not all had been peaceful between the cowboys and natives, so he decided to move immediately out of the sheepmen's country toward a permanent range around the canyon of the Palo Duro. Before departing, however, he made a treaty with the sheepmen by which he agreed to forsake the Canadian Valley, if they, in turn, would stay away from the canyon.

An old Mexican trader named Martínez, familiar with the Indian trails, was hired to pilot the party down into the Palo Duro. Early in November they arrived at the mouth of the gorge. They entered the canyon by way of the old course marked by the Comanches—over a path so narrow and rugged that hours were consumed pushing the cattle down in single file and all equipment and provisions had to be carried on muleback.

A flat lying toward the south side was chosen as the site for the headquarters. There, on a verdant strip of land, adorned by rich-hued cliffs and cedars of green, watered by a tiny stream that trickled from ledges above, protected by walls rising to a height of a thousand feet and uninhabited except for buffalo and black bear, was established the first ranch in the Texas Panhandle. As if in challenge to the virgin country that surrounded it, it was called the Old Home Ranch.

As soon as Goodnight had settled his cattle and men on the new range, he returned again to Colorado to arrange for his wife, who was anxiously awaiting the time when she might join him. It was during this trip that he was introduced to John G. Adair, with whom he formed the partnership that resulted in the JA Ranch.

Adair was an Irishman of great wealth who had forsworn the dignified career in diplomacy for which he had been educated to engage in the more exciting game of finance. During a visit to America in 1866, he established a brokerage firm in New York for the purpose of reloaning, at the high rate of 10 percent, the large sums of British capital available to him for 4 percent.

During one of his numerous business trips to this country, he met and married a widow, Mrs. Ritchie, who, as Cornelia Wadsworth, was a member of one of America's most prominent families. After their marriage, he and his bride returned to Ireland to establish a permanent residence on his estate there, but they continued, nevertheless, to spend about half of each year in the United States, traveling and attending to financial matters. In 1874, they journeyed to the region of the Platte to hunt buffalo, a sport very popular with the leisure class of that time. During this expedition Adair became so interested in the western frontier that he determined to move his brokerage headquarters to Denver and, as soon as he was established there, to make connections that would enable him to enter the cattle business on an extensive scale.

But, like Hughes, he found that his project required the services of a partner familiar with the country and capable of taking over the active management, for, like most Englishmen engaged in ranching in the United States, he did not intend to become an American citizen. Upon inquiring for such a man, he was given Goodnight's name, and an introduction between the two was arranged. The result was the formation of the firm of Goodnight and Adair, a partnership which, for the purpose of gain, fused into seemingly impossible union two unblendable elements: one, the typical frontiersman molded by the "rough-hewn surroundings of a pioneer life," and the other, an Old World sophisticate unsuited in every way to the new and democratic West.

An agreement was quickly reached; Adair was to furnish the money and Goodnight was to buy, develop, and manage the ranch at a yearly salary of twenty-five hundred dollars. At the termination of the five-year contract, there was to be a division by which Goodnight would receive one-third of the land, cattle, and horses, after reimbursing Adair for the one-third of the money invested by him, with the addition of 10 percent interest; Adair would receive the other two-thirds of the land. At Goodnight's suggestion, Adair's connected initials JA were chosen as the brand.

Only one year from the time he had set out with his first herd from Colorado to the Palo Duro, Goodnight was ready to start on his third trip. This time he was accompanied by his wife, who refused to be separated from him any longer, regardless of hardship, and by his new partner and his wife. They took with them four loads of freight, which included building materials and supplies for six months, and a hundred head of high-grade Durham bulls. Mrs. Goodnight drove one of the wagons, and Mrs. Adair rode horseback during the entire four hundred miles of the trip. They arrived at the Palo Duro headquarters in the late spring of 1877.

The Irish couple remained in Texas only long enough to hunt a few buffalo and then departed, leaving Goodnight in full charge. Adair, with his British accent, European ideas, and a hat worn at a rakish angle, was none too popular with the cowboys on the ranch; and his wife, like many Americans in similar circumstances, after marriage affected manners more British than those of the native born. Both were in the Panhandle so seldom that they were almost legendary figures. However, a wealthy widow in later years, she occasionally appeared in person, and, after the grand manner in which she was accustomed to live, thrilled the vicinity with her foreign guests, fifteen trunks, and courtly retinue of maids, butlers, and secretaries.

Goodnight and Adair's first contract limited the size of the herd and the amount of acreage to be purchased, but under Adair's instructions additional land was soon being bought right and left, usually at prices ranging from twenty to thirty-five cents an acre, sometimes in blocks of over 100,000 acres. At the dissolution of the partnership, sometime after Adair's death, there were 99,000 head of cattle grazing a range of over a million acres, 600,000 of which Goodnight and Adair owned.

The original cattle placed in the Palo Duro, with the addition of the high-grade Durham bulls brought on the third trip, formed the nucleus from which developed the enormous JA herd. As the Durhams proved unsuitable to the country, they were soon discarded for the finest longhorns on the market. These thrived but, because of their build, never developed into flesh; to offset this condition, in 1882, some thoroughbred Hereford stock was added, and out of the combination of colored, Durham, longhorn, and Hereford came the finest breed ever raised in the Panhandle—roan steers much heavier even than those of today.

Very early, different camps were established. John Mann, the foreman, and Joe Horn lived at Deep Lake. Mac Good and Jim Campbell were on Mexican Creek, and Johnny Campbell and Johnny Monroe were at the head of Mulberry Creek. In 1879 the headquarters was moved from the canyon to the top of its mouth, twenty-five miles from the original location. It was there that the big ranch house was built for the visiting Adairs and resident managers. There also were constructed dugouts for the boys, a blacksmith shop, mess house, corral, and barns. The outfit had grown to include more than thirty men, some stationed at line camps and others helping to run the two wagons, all part of a smooth-running organization, which, after practically one hundred years, although much diminished in size, is still a monument of life and blood to the men whose visions conceived it.

There is an old Welsh proverb that states, "There are three foundations for genius: the gift of the gods, man's exertions, and events to suit." Tall and powerfully built, Goodnight possessed, first of all, the fearless spiritual hardihood that springs, as a rule, only from perfect health and a gigantic body. He was abounding in vitality, intelligent, a keen observer of every manifestation of nature, and a gifted judge of men and cattle. His outstanding characteristics were physical endurance, an aptitude for work, self-confidence, and determination. It was a well-intentioned Providence that placed one so endowed among the ideal surroundings of the frontier where each was a law unto himself and might was right, where the man who succeeded was the one who marked a trail for success and blazed it straight to the end by hewing down and brushing aside, as he did the undergrowth at his feet, all obstacles, human or otherwise, that arose to obstruct his path or retard his progress.

He was the essence of rugged individualism, the type of pioneer most admired by Americans. And he still retained two of his primitive predecessors' dominant attributes: to a marked degree he had the Indian's kinship with nature and the adventurer's love of excitement and of the personal freedom possible only in unpopulated areas. He had no knowledge of the laws of cause and effect, no interest in the advancement of mankind in general. He and his kind laid the foundation for an empire, it is true, without conscious effort, while engrossed with their own selfish concerns. It is difficult to know whether Goodnight was a big-hearted "diamond in the rough" whose uncouth exterior gave little evidence of the keen intelligence and upright character underneath, a great man with a simple nature and the frontier's foremost stockman, as his chief champion described him, or an overbearing master, unpopular with the cowboys, who was the finest fellow in the world only as long as one did exactly as he desired and whose one ambition was to rule the plains country (and who, at one time, came near to doing it).

Concerning his wife there was never a question. To one and all she stood for everything that is admirable in womanhood, this gentle "lady" from Tennessee. Set by circumstances amid surroundings too uncongenial to her highstrung, sensitive temperament, she was dashed and buffeted by the winds of western life until her frail body broke. But to the end, she remained the beloved "Aunt Molly" of every cowboy who had ever known her.

When Mrs. Goodnight arrived at her new home in the Palo Duro, she discovered her nearest woman neighbor to be living upon the Canadian River—across an intervening distance of seventy-five miles. There, during the months between the establishment of the Old Home Ranch and the JA, the lucky accident of a swollen stream and a scattered herd had caused Thomas Sherman Bugbee to stop among the breaks at the mouth of the canyon later named in his honor. There, in a dugout surrounded by buffalo, ten days by wagon from the nearest town, he stopped with his little family to found the Panhandle's second ranch. His wife was only a blue-eyed, quick-tempered, laughing girl, so small she could stand under her husband's outstretched arm, but a perfect complement to the big, steady, taciturn pioneer. Together they brought to success the Quarter Circle T.

When Goodnight and Bugbee advanced onto the virgin region of Northwest Texas, their methods were much the same as those employed by all cowmen on appropriating a range where nature provided feed for their herds without labor or expense. In a country so endless as to both grazing resources and size, the initial moves of the pioneer were to establish headquarters at any advantageous location and then to claim every adjacent acre and those even far beyond.

On the appearance of a second settler, a division was made without argument; with the coming of others, the district was, of necessity, further divided with each individual keeping good faith, as a rule, and respecting at all times the range boundaries so arbitrarily defined. Later, in case of actual purchase, the procedure was either to locate certificates previously acquired or to buy direct from the railroads.

Because large tracts of these public lands often had no living water and were worthless when cut off from access to it, it was necessary to own outright only enough acreage to control the water rights on the desired area. Thus, through the purchase of a comparatively small tract, the possession of an extensive range was automatically assured without cost. Imagine the opportunity!

An added advantage was the fact that during these same years the cattle industry itself was steadily and swiftly climbing to a high peak. With the discovery of a process of refrigeration that made possible the shipment of beef across the ocean, consumption increased by leaps and bounds. The effect of war prices still prevailed to some extent. In consequence, the Panhandle stockman was offered on one hand an expanding and rising market and on the other a range so luxuriant that it required only ten acres for each cow (today, with less rain, the required acreage varies with climatic conditions and artificial feeding is often used). It was a system that guaranteed, for every acre purchased at an approximate cost of twenty cents, the right to an average of ten additional ones free. Was it then so astounding that during the years of their

first contract Goodnight and Adair sometimes had an annual profit of 70 percent, or that cattlemen from everywhere rushed in after them to reap the reward of a land that made such success possible?

CHAPTER 5

The Open Range

(The Stockman and His Kingdom)

BY the early 1880's there were scattered over the plains the numerous herds by which men were to rise to easy wealth. It was a world all its own, this empire of free grass, and its capital was Tascosa, a typical boom town characterized by bad men, prostitutes, guns, and whiskey, in perfect accord with the relentless harshness of the country and the unstable nature of the ephemeral era that spawned it.

A colorful aggregation of humanity peopled this town of Tascosa: cowboys celebrating with six-shooters, señoritas in lace mantillas, priests in their sober cassocks, university graduates, gamblers, and desperadoes whose chief gathering place was John Cone's long adobe building, which conveniently housed his store, a bar, a dance hall, and some bedrooms, and was located in a district that had fittingly come to be known as Hog Town. It was a pleasant arrangement that enabled the customer to enter through the door of respectability, as it were; then, if he so desired, to pass on to the less taxing negotiations by the bar and from there to the dance hall just beyond, from which, if he was lucky, he made his exit with empty pockets and on unsteady legs—if not, with face covered and feet first in the arms of sympathizing but unchastened companions in vice. The queen of the district—of Hog Town—was Rowdy Kate; some of the other girls went by such descriptive names as Ragtime Annie, Drowsy Dollie, Crippled Callie, Boxcar Jane, Panhandle Nan, Fickle Flossie, and Midnight Rose. It was a place where officers of the law paid small heed to what went on, where every man made his own rule of conduct and backed it with a forty-five.[1]

The cemetery was a fenced-in cow pasture, appropriately called Boothill, for its occupants were, for the most part, men who had met death not from natural causes but while still ambulatory and wearing boots. The most famous of these now permanent recumbents were the three "fighting cowboys," actually little more than children, whom the LS outfit had employed to help settle the

[1] John Arnot, "My Recollections of Tascosa Before and After the Coming of the Law," *Panhandle-Plains Historical Review* 6 (1933), 63.

only labor and management conflict in the history of the free-grass era.

The town's more dignified dances, aside from the fiestas of upper-class Mexicans, were held at the Exchange Hotel, where the dust from the floor rolled up in clouds as the fun progressed and the fiddler often had to shout, "Everybody outside," and set aside his musical instrument long enough to "sprinkle down."

The "eating house" belonged to Mrs. Betty Trube and was a small abode where sanctuary was offered one and all for the mere price of a meal. She was a huge woman, as strong as a man, and wore at her waist a six-shooter which she did not hesitate to brandish at any person showing signs of disturbing the peace of her establishment.

The best-known gambler was a jovial Irishman from Dodge City, who owned the livery stable but spent most of his days roaming the nearby hills with his hunting dogs and all of his nights at the gambling tables. His partner in chance, so the legend goes, was the shrewdest monte dealer in the West, a tiny, beautiful girl known as "Frenchy" or "Creole Mary." Night after night she sat among the sports dressed in her spangled blouse, patch-work skirt, and red shoes, with rarely a word to anyone except her talking bird hanging in a cage at the back of the room. This parrot was said to have cost one hundred and fifty dollars and was one of the numerous gifts that Mickey gave to the girl he loved.

But the most famous man ever to tread the streets of Tascosa was William E. Bonney of New York and New Mexico. Bonney, or Billy the Kid, as he was more commonly called, made his living by stealing cattle from the big ranches to supply the government agents with beef for the forts and reservations. Legend says he killed a man for every year of his life before he himself met a premature death at the age of twenty-one. But be that as it may, he was a peaceable, gentlemanly boy when in town, well liked by the men with whom he had no business dealings and a hero to the ladies, whom he always treated with the greatest courtesy.

It was Billy the Kid who presented the town's first physician with the beautiful pony on which he traveled the roads around Tascosa. Dr. Hoyt was inveigled into coming to Tascosa by the ardent sales talk of someone who assured the future town doctor that a thriving city filled with invalids was waiting for him. Upon his arrival Hoyt discovered the only sick persons to be a few impoverished Mexicans with smallpox. When he had nursed these back to health, he found himself without further employment and was forced to forsake the practice of

medicine for the more certain, if less congenial, job of cow-punching. One day he was called in to dress the wounds of Billy the Kid and, having performed to the satisfaction of the injured man, was offered a beautiful saddle horse named "Dandy Dick" in payment. He liked the horse immensely but was reluctant to accept a gift of possibly doubtful ownership. Seeing his hesitation, the Kid smiled and said, "I'll fix that all right. I'll give you a bill of sale which will release you from any responsibility." After that, the doctor took the horse and rode it with much pleasure, although time proved what he had suspected from the first, that it was stolen property and, worse than that, had belonged at the time of the theft to a sheriff in New Mexico.

Such was Tascosa, the cowboy capital, destined, like Adobe Walls, Fort Elliott, and Mobeetie, to make its contribution to the history of the West and then to pass into obscurity. It was the contribution of the earlier ones to clear the way, that of Tascosa to lay the foundation for the economic structure of a civilization yet to come.

But by one of the inexplicable contradictions of life, the spiritual qualities necessary for the survival of that civilization were to come from a totally dissimilar atmosphere and from a gentler breed of men, men not characterized by spectacular exploits or revolutionary discoveries but by a simple philosophy that motivated their commonplace lives, men so unsuited to the harsh frontier that more often than not they themselves were conquered by their surroundings. In the end, they, too, like those before them, only added their bit to the sum total that is the West of today and then passed on.

To the south and east of Tascosa lay the district of Donley. Across the center of its fertile prairies ran the Salt Fork of the Red River, and along one side and most of its upper boundary extended the sloping and steep walls of cap rock, forming a break against the icy cold and the bitter winds that swept down from the High Plains above.

Upon a stretch of this country during the last of the 1870's was established a ranch called the Quarter Circle Heart. Although its herd reached a total of many thousand head, it is in respects other than as a cattle outfit that it assumes importance in this narrative. Its brand is remembered not as cattle identification but as the symbol of a man and a range—of the founder and the setting of the Panhandle's first colonization scheme. The colony was the harbinger of a coming era in which some of the grasslands were to be ploughed under and the trails traversing them were to sink from sight beneath fields of cotton, corn, and wheat.

The route by which the plains were finally reached

was a long and circuitous one, destined to bring to defeat a life that promised much in the beginning. In 1866 a Methodist bishop assigned to Arkansas a young "trial preacher" by the name of Lewis Henry Carhart. It was the first "charge" in a clerical career begun in specific payment to God for assistance rendered at the time of a near-fatal illness of the young Carhart during a term of service in the Union Army.

So propitious were the circumstances surrounding the ex-soldier's advent into the ministry that there is no reckoning the heights to which he might have climbed had not unusual circumstances diverted him from his original course. As a graduate of both the theological department of Northwestern University and the Garrett Biblical Institute, he was well prepared intellectually; his family was a prominent one in the Methodist denomination, and personally he was endowed with zeal and every other attribute conducive to success in the ministry. He possessed good looks, charm of manner, a spontaneous affection for people, and an inward fire of conviction that reduced to naught any will or opinion opposed to his own. He also had a genius for leadership. Unfortunately, this genius lay largely in his powers of persuasion rather than in any real ability to guide or any unusual depth of character, and, as a result, he was not always able to dis-

charge the responsibilities and honors thrust upon him.

As the years passed, he steadily and rapidly advanced in the church from "trial preacher" to "full connections" —to deacon, to elder, to secretary of the conference, and so on, until in 1877, he was in Texas presiding over the Denison District and in charge of the Sherman pastorate.

At that time the Methodist church, like all else in the state, was in the pioneering stage, and its problem was not so much a matter of spiritual development as of physical survival. Consequently, the man who best served the denomination was the one who devoted all his efforts to the establishment of a basic organization and left to those who were to follow the task of instilling spiritual values. Carhart's chief duty, and he knew it, was not to convert individuals to the virtuous life but to convert districts to Methodism.

Therefore, as soon as he settled in Sherman, Carhart undertook the building of the first brick church in town. As an aid to the difficult problem of financing the project, someone suggested the purchase of "scrip" for resale to prospective settlers at a substantial profit. The minister heartily approved the idea. He had long been interested in land and in the development of the Texas frontier and had even gone on a tour once for the Immigration Board at Austin to lecture to his northern friends on the advantages of a state where the sun never failed to shine.

Spurred on by the enthusiasm of their leader, the good women of the congregation baked, sewed, and gave bazaars in order to raise the initial fund. Soon all preliminaries were settled, the scrip was bought, and Carhart was charged with turning it into cash—an easy assignment for one whose powers of salesmanship made failure impossible, whether the article happened to be stock in a life after death or acreage in a less celestial realm. Needless to say, the church soon stood complete, free from debt and ready for use.

All this occurred at a time when moneyed interests in the East were beginning to turn their attention to the Texas Northwest, and it so happened that Carhart's wife was the sister of one Alfred Sully, a wealthy financier connected with the investment firm of Austin and Corbett of New York. As official adviser to the institution's customers and a heavy speculator himself, Alfred Sully was familiar and all kinds of bonds and stocks, Texas land certificates included.

Simultaneously with his introduction to the benefits of scrip by his brother-in-law, Sully came by chance into a large block of Panhandle land paper. With the first report of Carhart's success, Sully's interest was aroused, and, as letter followed letter, he began to regard as a real asset that

which before had been a mere stock market commodity, especially as many of his northern acquaintances and fellow financiers shared Carhart's enthusiasm for the new country.

Certainly the land seemed rich in promise and ripe for development. The minister's experience gave him a practical knowledge of the region, and his position in the church assured a widely extended acquaintance; Sully possessed the scrip, the financial backing, and influence. Together, the two men—eastern capitalist and local promoter —could form a partnership that might prove vastly advantageous to both, or so the broker figured. Thus was the idea of founding a colony in the Panhandle conceived, but which of the men actually originated the idea or made the initial suggestion is not known.

Of one thing, however, there is no doubt. The scheme was most agreeable in every respect to Carhart. In all fairness it must be said that it did not appeal to him solely for material reasons, nor was his intention ever to forsake the church. He was a man consumed by ambitions and energies for which the usual ministerial routine failed to offer sufficient outlet. He would continue his activities but in a country that gave more scope to one of his missionary tendencies. Out here on the frontier he would found a colony in which there would be churches and schools and temperance, through which mighty mediums he would lead a heathen land to his northern Methodist God. Furthermore, he had brought to Texas vivid memories of a place where the weather in winter reached a temperature too low for the thermometer to register, and he genuinely wished to share with his less fortunate friends the comfort of the sunny state of his adoption.

So, with all haste, he persuaded Con Haney, a former classmate, to "supply" for him in Sherman and, having thus temporarily freed himself from active duty, made ready for a departure west that he might locate as quickly as possible the lands that were to form the basis of speculation for his brother-in-law's scheme.

Accompanied by another clergyman, W. A. Allen, the husband of one of his sisters, he set out, traveling first to Dodge City by train, then overland to Mobeetie, where Mark Huselby supplied a hack and driver for the remainder of the journey. He had heard from buffalo hunters about the fine water and fertility of a certain region below the cap rock; the party, therefore, headed in that direction and continued until the Salt Fork was reached and crossed.

There, in May, 1878, by the side of the big lake lying to the south of the river, the first piece of land was located. Carhart and his surveyors chose wisely and apparently

with full familiarity with the possibilities of free grass. Although there were but nineteen patents registered that first year, those few were so phrased that they practically appropriated through water control all of Carroll Creek and parts of Spring and Record—a fertile strip in the heart of a range that in time came to include 343 sections of land to extend, east and west, from the present town of Giles to Goodnight, and, south and north, from the JA fence past McClellan Creek and over into Gray County for eleven miles.

Although the plan was to operate both in land and in cattle, the primary object was to use the property for colonization. Therefore, the next step after defining the boundaries was to establish a central settlement. The site selected was a flat lying near the junction of Carroll Creek and the Salt Fork. Above the creek was a high bluff over which ran the road to Mobeetie and Fort Elliott. In another direction chalk-gray and clay-red mounds rose, mound beyond mound, to join the prairies that led to Tascosa. A half-mile away to the south there stretched the wide bed of the river whose trickling stream gave little indication of the mighty torrent that on occasion roared there. During rainy springs, daisies and "Indian blankets" covered the hills, and primroses, winecups, morning glories, and cone flowers made a profusion of color. Tall cottonwoods grew in clumps along the "draws," forming shelters of green leaves during times of drouth. Sagebrush and mesquites, with their bean-pods hanging conveniently low, dotted the endless drifts of sand. On bright days the far-off horizon drew near, and, on the nights when it shone, the moon floated like a luminous balloon just beyond reach. There amid tarantulas, rattlesnakes, lobo-wolves, wind, and sand, on October 1, 1878, Carhart set up his Christian colony and named it Clarendon in honor of his wife.

CHAPTER 6

The Christian Colony: Clarendon

As soon as the townsite was laid out, construction was begun on the group of houses around which it was hoped a city would grow. First, in accordance with the spiritual purpose of the project, a one-room frame building, to serve as a combined church and school, was erected, next, a larger structure of adobe for the personal use of the minister, his wife, and two children, and last, a rock hotel of a size sufficient to accommodate the number of early settlers Carhart hoped to attract. As all freight was hauled from Dodge City, lumber was not only scarce but prohibitive in price; consequently, the building materials most commonly used were native rock, handmade adobe bricks, picket saplings, and blocks of sod. The excitement was great when the Bobbits drove in to build with the assistance of Kiah May, their freighter, the colony's first homestead, a hut of cedar logs and adobe.

Quickly other simple structures sprang up on the flat. Several families accompanied the minister on his second trip to the western prairies. Like almost all his colonists, they were Northerners who had known him in Iowa, visionary individuals who, under the influence of his religious fervor, had left comfortable homes to take up a life for which they were suited by neither temperament nor training. Numerous single men who had been buffalo hunters and some few married couples were already living in dugouts along Carroll Creek. Many of these moved into the colony at once, the women for companionship, and the men to have the advantage of a definite center of trade. The hotel was put in the charge of a German couple named Heffelbower; nearby was the adobe home and office of Stanhope McClelland; Faun Bartlett built a wagon yard by the blacksmith shop of Jim Burdick, and Major Van Horn, who operated the sutler's concession at Fort Elliott, opened a small branch supply store. On a corner of the main street stood the bootshop of Ed Corbett.

On the top of Eagle Hill, the high mound from which the Indians once signaled to distant tribes, a rude refuge was thrown together by forming with a breastwork of rocks and mud an enclosure large enough to accommodate all the inhabitants in case of Indian attack. Openings for guns were left around the edges, and extra ammunition was stored in caches close by. However, the anticipated Indian attack did not occur, and in time the hill was put to a more useful purpose. On holidays and other special occasions, from the tip of a tall pole, an American flag waved proudly over the humble settlement below.

In its aggregation of humanity were types as opposed as the two poles, with George Osborn, a buffalo hunter, at one extreme, and, at the other, gentle old Professor Combs, who had abandoned schoolteaching to invest the meager savings of a lifetime in cows, that he and his wife might enjoy immediate affluence and the leisurely old age of the landed gentry. He was a "character," like so many men in the new colony. After his huge brand KOMZ was applied, there was little to be seen of the rest of the calf. Having turned his cattle loose on the Heart range, he dismissed them from his mind and concentrated on pursuits more in keeping with his temperament and training. He loved music passionately and spent many months fashioning a violin for himself from cedar logs. When his health permitted and his chores had not proved too tiring, he would settle himself after supper for an evening of sacred hymns and by their simple melodies would transport his spirit to the gentler scene of bygone days.

The town's two pretentious houses stood far back on the creek and belonged to Tom Morrison, who operated the Baby Doll Ranch, and to J. H. Parks, a practicing surveyor from Illinois, whose wife, Vashta, was a relative of Lew Wallace and an intimate friend of Abraham Lincoln's family. With her busy little ways, Vashta Parks was soon one of the town's best-known inhabitants. To paraphrase the words of the Bible, "Wherever two or three were gathered together, there was she in the midst of them," sympathetic, helpfully interested in every detail of the life of all who came within the bounds of her acquaintance, not only willing but always eager to lend an efficient and helping hand, a typical clubwoman of today born unfortunately too soon, in a time when organizing missionary societies and officiating at childbirth were the only outlets beyond the home for the female with executive ability.

Stanhope McClelland, like Parks also a surveyor, was a Virginian who had drifted to Texas in search of employment. While in Bonham, visiting a classmate with whom he had graduated from the Virginia Military Institute, he was offered a job on the Gunter and Munson crew bound for the Canadian River district. As he liked Northwest Texas, he stayed on after the departure of his fellow workers, making a living first in one way, then another. Soon after the establishment of the colony, he was appointed state surveyor and took up residence in town to resume the profession for which he had been trained.

All the colonists acquired land, some more, some less, and many of them settled on sections out from town—among them the Hassers, the Stamms, the Wagners, and the Holdens.

It is difficult for those accustomed to the conveniences of an industrial age to visualize the primitive dwellings with which most of the pioneers had to content themselves. But the frontier housewife was often a genius at the art of homemaking and could perform miracles with what little she had to work with. One of this kind was Mrs. Taber, whose husband had taken over a dugout at the foot of a steep hill by the side of Carroll Creek.

Old Seman Taber was a small, stooped, bewhiskered man, unobtrusive and mild-mannered but very industrious. How he happened upon the plains no one knew, for he was a Yankee by birth and a puddler by trade and apparently in no financial difficulty. In spite of his alien temperament and the semi-aridity of the land, he set himself to raise fruit and vegetables where heretofore only mesquite and sagebrush had grown. In a few years his orchard and garden began to bear, and in the role of the county's first experimental farmer and the town's only greengrocer he prospered.

Previous to that time, he had been content to be a bachelor, but affluence and the needs of his declining years wrought a change in him, and with the assistance of a matrimonial agency, he began a quest for a mate. A bride arrived in due time, a friendly little widow, Mrs. Helen Moore. After a few days' sojourn at the home of Professor and Mrs. Combs, to give herself time to look the situation over, she and Taber were married. Somewhat unexpectedly, they lived happily together until death severed the union.

Their dugout had once belonged to Straight, a buffalo hunter, and, like all those on Carroll Creek, had a roof on a level with the hill behind and walls of sod slabs. It was, as dugouts went, a commodious dwelling, with three rooms arranged so as to open one into the other. To prevent the untidiness of scaling dirt, gunnysacks were stretched across the walls and held in place by tightly tacked cheese cloth. On small drygoods boxes carefully fitted together to serve as shelves were the couple's few prized books and knickknacks. The ceiling and floor were made of wide planks.

The mail-order wife was not only a very good woman but neat as a pin and an excellent cook. Everyone enjoyed her hospitality on occasion, and the young people, especially, liked on sunny days to walk out to visit her, and, after having feasted on her tea and wine and cake, to examine the souvenirs and knickknacks she had tucked around in her cozy sod house.

To the north of the Tabers, on McClellan Creek, was the S. B. Barton horse ranch, probably the only one of its kind in the entire region. Barton was an Ohioan who had followed the buffalo for many years in the company of Buck Henson and Bill Lampton, said to have been members of Quantrill's outlaw—"guerrilla" was the term used in those days—band. When the hunting was ended, he joined a state surveying gang as chainbearer, and, by preference, took his three-dollar-a-day wage in land. After acquiring by this slow method scrip for several sections, he settled on the part of the creek that controlled the water supply for a large area—furnishing an interesting example of opportunity offered enterprising youth a century ago.

Bill Ross was another who lived out on the creek. He was a real frontiersman, as familiar with the ways of the plains as any Indian. He could smell a deer a mile away or tell from animal tracks if water was near. He was about 6'6", powerfully built, and weighed close to 250 pounds, with not an ounce of surplus flesh. He was so strong that he could catch a wild Spanish mule by the nose and ear and hold it alone until it was harnessed. He spoke in a booming voice that pealed out like a bass horn; when he addressed his team, he could be heard a mile away.

Every few months Dempsey Forrest drove into town to pick up supplies. His business was catching wild mustangs, and his outfit consisted of a wagon or two, ten strong boys, and an endless amount of rope. He dressed like Daniel Boone in a deerskin suit and wore his hair long. Besides the gun which he always carried, he had pistols at his waist and bowie knives stuck in the tops of his boots. In winter he wrapped his feet and ankles in gunnysacks for added warmth. His appearance, as a result, was ferocious; actually, he was the mildest kind of fellow whose honesty, big heart, and sagacity earned him the respect of everyone for many prairie miles around. Such were the first inhabitants of the little Clarendon colony.

During the eighteen months following the patenting of the first few sections, Carhart devoted most of his time to his interests here in West Texas. As the town grew, so did his enthusiasm, until, with no intent to falsify or exaggerate but convinced by his own oratory of the reality of the mirage city that arose before him on the horizon of his desire, he came to think and talk of Clarendon as the future metropolis of the plains, where someday steamboats would stop to dock as they churned across the populous Panhandle upon the deep and wide waters of the Salt Fork.

The Christian Colony: Clarendon 55

CHAPTER 7

The New Era

(For God, School, and Temperance)

IN just a few months the bare, sandy stretch had been transformed into the home ground of a small colony of happy, hopeful people and a trading-post that promised to become the business center of the Panhandle's most fertile area. The foundation had been well laid; the next step was to acquaint the world with the colony's existence and to call attention to the material advantages and possibilities of the land surrounding it. Heretofore Carhart had used personal contacts, posters, and church periodicals as his means of advertising. Having decided that at this point favorable propaganda could best be disseminated through a regional and personally conducted publication, he set about to establish a newspaper.

The attending circumstances would have proved too discouraging to a man of less dauntless spirit, but whatever the minister's deficiencies, he was never lacking in energy or determination. No obstacle subject to removal by effort on his part obstructed for long the path of his ambitions. Although he himself had to take time from many conflicting duties to act as manager and editor-in-chief, it was only a matter of weeks until an issue after the manner of the following appeared in circulation:

CLARENDON NEWS[1]

Clarendon, Texas

Aug. 2, 1879
Sherman, Texas
Rev. L. H. Carhart,
Editor and Business Manager
James H. Parks, Local Editor

Christianity   Education   Temperance
Civilization Westward

A monthly journal devoted to the settlement and upbuilding of Northwestern Texas

Published the first of each month at Clarendon, Donley County, Texas   50¢ a year

[1] The newspaper was called the *Clarendon Panhandle News* for a time, and so far as is known its owners (or managers) were L. H. Carhart, Ed Carhart, Charlie Kimball, William Jesse Grant, A. M. Beeville, and Joe Warren.

Local Items[2]

S. B. Barton, formerly of Ohio, says he never saw, even in his own state, a better setting of corn than is found in Mr. Heffelbower's field this year.

Mr. J. T. Rice, formerly of Massachusetts, a harness maker by trade, is a welcome addition to our midst.

A barber chair is among our recent acquisitions.

No whiskey forever at Clarendon.

The two new mail routes will be in operation from Elliott to Henrietta and Ft. Griffin by October first.

E. Burlingame, Esquire, of Clarendon, has charge of a new freight line. Six splendid mules will be sure to be in on time with such a hand.

Mr. Babcock, a stock-grower, is coming to educate his children.

A good stable can be built quickly and cheaply of sod.

Special Notice:

I expect to be at Clarendon with my family by August 15th. Let all correspondence be addressed to me there via Dodge City, Kansas. Let monies, as far as possible, be sent by draft on New York, payable to order. Postal orders, when used, should be made payable at Sherman

[2] The author was able to locate only one copy of the *Clarendon News* (August 2, 1879), so for some items the source was various issues of the *Tascosa Pioneer*, another frontier paper published during the 1880's.

but enclosed to us at Clarendon, as above. Our post-office at Clarendon is not a money-order office.

Such was the beginning of the Panhandle's first and oldest newspaper. Down through the years it continued without interruption. Many publishers came and went and are forgotten. The town moved, and the paper's name was changed, but through it all the *Clarendon News* succeeded in appearing fairly close to schedule.

The assembling of copy for each issue was a task of some proportion, as news on the frontier was scarce, difficult to procure, and more often than not of a nature unsuited to the purpose of the paper. This accomplished, the copy was sent all the way to Oshkosh, Wisconsin, for printing; the papers were returned by train to Sherman for distribution among prospective settlers in the North and to the subscribers in Clarendon. The typesetting in Oshkosh was done by a cousin of the minister, Dr. J. W. Carhart, whose chief assistant was his son, Ed, a boy who, although only seventeen years of age, was very efficient at his trade.

When the long-distance method of getting out the paper was found too impracticable to be continued, the job of resident publisher was offered to Ed Carhart. A proposition so flattering to one of his years required little persuasion, and he was soon on the train for Texas to assume a prestigious position possibly at no other time in the history of Texas held by a newspaperman so young.

As soon as Ed and his new printing outfit were installed for business in the shop built especially for him out of cedar saplings before his arrival, he changed the paper to a weekly and advanced the price to two dollars a year. Because his printing press was a flat-bed hand press and turned out only a page at a time, and because he had to be reporter, editor, typesetter, and printer, it was an achievement to publish regularly every seven days even a sheet twelve by fourteen inches in size. When his first issue appeared in July, 1880, the entire colony was proud, and so was he.

The following year Ed Carhart sold the paper to Charlie Kimball, a man from the East who had arrived in the vicinity with the Combs family. Ed Carhart continued to work on the paper for a short while. In order that the weekly might have full-size newspaper format, a Washington hand press was installed. The new equipment made larger quarters necessary, and the shop was moved to one of the lean-tos that had been added to the minister's former house to convert it into business property. Lewis Henry Carhart continued to live there when in town, but without his family; his wife disliked the country and after one or two trips refused to endure the hardships and loneliness of the place named in her honor.

The paper's advertisements were chiefly of guns, wagons, harness, and patent medicines; its editorials ranged from ethics to life in the Panhandle. Among the titles were "The Debt to Mother," "The Dignity of Farm Life," "Rain and Civilization," and "Five Days without Water" (this last being an account of the experience of some men lost upon the plains). When someone died, the caption above the obituary was appropriate to the occasion and reminded those who survived that "dust returned to dust" and "ashes to ashes." When a business failed, it was "another to the wall." Now and then a cattle brand appeared with the warning: "Whoever handles these cattle without authority will catch Hell." News items were of a most personal nature and presented a graphic picture of the simple life of the pioneer and the gradual coming of civilization to the frontier.

Blow, soft breezes . . . the heaviest storm of wind known to the residents arose Monday morning before day and for twelve long hours made the old bones rattle. As it was from the north every movable object out of doors at once emigrated southward. One could take a sheltered position and see boxes, barrels, cans, boards, cottonwood limbs, and occasional pieces of house-roofing go whirling by to the river. Volumes and clouds of sand filled the air at all times. Panhandle soil shifted its location rapidly; sand and dust and gravel left deep holes in some quarters to pile mountain high in others. Under doors and through cracks and around windows swept wind and dirt. Light buildings yielded to the first blasts, into which papers and rags and leaves and straw and twigs and earth poured. Two houses lost their shingle roofing and even some of the flat dirt roofs were made penetrable by the later sunshine. The short-order restaurant could do no business in a frame building so gave neither breakfast nor dinner.

Sunday was another one of the blustery and dusty days of which we average about two a week.

A moonlight night in the Panhandle and especially this part is one of the wondrously beautiful things of creation.

A good rain on the style of the one old Noah had would wake things up somewhat just now.

From Mobeetie comes the report of prairie fires doing considerable damage on the range while this section is enjoying rain in abundance.

The classic Salt Fork rose up on an undignified "tear" last Thursday without any apparent reason.

The plumming season is almost over.

The mosquito blows his melodious horn nightly and the indications are that the sad-eyed, silvery-voiced, sharp-toothed pest will be too plentiful in these parts this year.

The musical frog keeps up the regular and entertaining play on his harmonica.

The big red ant gets in his fine work these days walking with easy dignity up the spine of the youngster who sits in his bed; serenely shoves his little stiletto up to the hilt; and the beauty of it is, he does it with the assurance of ownership. And from sitting in an ant's hill, the youngster after that sits in the seat of the mournful.

The heel-fly has returned into the country numerously and can be found doing business at the old stand.

The prairie dog is receiving a good deal of attention lately from press and people. Legislatures in one or two states and territories are paying a regular reward for the killing of these little pests and the people of Northwest Texas are beginning to appeal to our law-makers. The Panhandle will never be successfully farmed while prairie dog towns extend hundreds of miles into and around it, for the agriculturists cannot fight this class of enemies with any prospect of coming out winner. They cut the growing crops to the ground in every instance where a farmer invades a section that they have previously filed on.

It is round-up season throughout the live-stock region.

Most of the stockmen report from their respective ranges that the spring calf crop is unusually large. Calf harvest is, of course, fairly over sometime since.

The number of cattle that have gone up the trail through our one County during the spring on their way north was said to be up to June 6, 89,297.

The manager of the LIT ranch a couple of weeks ago discharged four of the boys whom he found gambling. An invariable rule of the company forbids gambling and carrying six-shooters about the ranch.

A sanguinary difficulty was threatened in town one day this week. Word had reached one of the boys that a business man had made undue reflection on his honesty and, Winchester in hand, he came to town to wipe the insult out in blood. But the officers were notified and, after a satisfactory explanation of just what had been said, the gentleman who was to have been made a target failed to appear and prosecute.

Mr. Satterwhite has the sub-contract for carrying the Clarendon and Tascosa mail and he made the first trip yesterday.

Numerous farms are now being opened up in all quarters of the Panhandle and they are all examples of the virtue of the soil for cereals, fruits, and vegetables. Wild plums and grapes grow plentifully and of superior quality.

A hunting party went out Sunday morning to take a round after deer and came in reporting the usual luck.

A small supply of buffalo meat was brought in by one of our neighbors yesterday and disposed of readily at the market. Bison steak is juicy and delicious but a rarity these days in the West. It used not to be thus.

Mr. ——— drives in now in fine style in his shining new hack. He is certainly letting off a lot of dignity lately.

It would seem near the time when the horse-racing season is on. We will have a Christmas tree, horse-races, balls and a general observance of holiday times.

The sums will yet aggregate nearly a couple of hundred dollars, it is thought, and all can enter who will.

In 1880 Carhart was assigned by the bishop to a church in Dallas, with one of the largest and most important congregations in the district. Without the assistance of his friend Haney, who was "supplying" for him in Sherman, and with his heavy pastoral duties in Dallas, he found his activities as a promoter as well as owner of a ranch he had started in Clarendon severely curtailed. He realized that if the colony were to be expanded and his personal financial interests to be safeguarded, he had to have a resident manager capable of assuming complete charge during his long and frequent absences from the Panhandle.

Carhart's forte was promotion rather than active management—something he had probably begun to suspect and which the succeeding years abundantly proved. The enterprise in Clarendon, both the colony and his ranch, had reached far greater magnitude than he had in his ignorance of practical affairs ever imagined it would; it required time and talents he was unable to provide. In desperation he wrote to his brother-in-law up north, Judge Benjamin Horton White, imploring him to move to Clarendon and become more or less his general manager.

At the time, Judge White, the husband of Carhart's sister Lottie, was a successful lawyer in Iowa. He had moved there for his health, but the expected benefits of the Iowa climate had proved an illusion, and Judge White's health had become worse. Convinced at last by Carhart's repeated assurances of the therapeutic values of the Texas sun and air, Judge White accepted the offer and made ready to move to Texas, not without some misgivings about the advisability of moving to the frontier.

The time consumed by the negotiations had covered a period of several months, during which Carhart felt himself more and more in need of help. And Judge White's actual move to Clarendon was still to come. Somehow, through his various church connections, Carhart had come to know another lawyer he thought might serve his purpose—at least until the arrival of his brother-in-law. By offering this lawyer, J. C. Murdock, among other, less material, inducements, a price above market value for his house and property in Henrietta, Carhart succeeded in persuading him to join the Clarendon colony and manage his ranch. Some weeks later, the lawyer, his wife, and their two children were settled in their new home, half a mile up Carroll Creek from the Tabers. They were the first of the families whose collective presence was to become a cultural influence of first importance in the development of the entire region.

For the moment, Carhart's anxieties were put to rest: Murdock was in charge of his ranch, and presently Judge White was to arrive in Clarendon to serve as guiding head and hand of the colony. The future promised to smile on Carhart's multiple widespread interests. The smile was not a permanent one, though.

As one pioneer described him, Carhart was a mixture of preacher, promoter, and actor, so good in each calling that he succeeded in none. There is no doubt that the emotional conflicts that went with his complex personality led in the end to disaster. But however great the complexity of the man, his outlook from first to last was that of the aristocrat.

It was one of the many enigmas of his character that his philosophy was founded on principles he himself often failed to follow. Although considerate and kind to those in his employ, he placed little reliance on the "common man." Great achievement, he felt, was always the result of a combination of moral and intellectual superiority. If a project were to succeed, the motivating influence must come from persons whose qualifications made leadership possible; therefore, it was his intention to attract to the colony only one class of individuals: people of education and of strict adherence to the Methodist faith.

The Murdocks were no exception to the rule. Their home was only a two-room dugout with a lean-to for their boy, Will, but an organ was a notable part of the furniture; the walls were neatly plastered with adobe and lined with books; carpets covered the floors, and window curtains thrashed back and forth in the dusty west wind. Their settling in marked the beginning of the spiritual conquest of the frontier.

The new manager's first move was to plant feed for the ranch horses. In the absence of fences, such crops as corn had to be guarded from the cattle, a job assigned to the young son. In payment, young Will received a yearling heifer, which he always insisted started the herd that gave him his start on the way to success; this was probably as true of Will Murdock as of many other cattlemen known to have risen from equally small beginnings.

When the White family finally arrived in Clarendon, Judge White was too weak to stand and had to be carried into his new home on a stretcher. However, the climate proved as efficacious as Carhart had predicted. In a few months the invalid was gradually able to assume the duties which he performed so faithfully for twenty years that he won the affection and respect of the entire Panhandle. Possessing the qualities Carhart lacked, Benjamin Horton White was a perfect complement to the other. For one thing, he was ideally suited by temperament and experience for the position he was to occupy. He had intelligence and business acumen and had received legal training, but, of even greater importance, he had the moral authority and broad humanity that even on the frontier singled him out for respect and unquestioned leadership.

It is interesting to note that today, after the passing of a century, Goodnight, whose wealth and power for a while made him "lord of the plains," lies in a grave provided only with the usual gravestone legend, whereas the dignified, gentle aristocrat, known to the West as the "Father of Donley County," rests under a marble shaft on which is inscribed: "None knew him but to love him."

When Donley County[3] was created in 1882 and Clarendon became the county seat, the rock hotel was converted into the courthouse. The change necessitated the building of a new hostelry, large enough to accommodate

[3] The organization of Donley County is described fully in chapter 12, below.

the increasing need of the community. Lumber was freighted in from Dodge City at three hundred dollars per thousand feet, to furnish the material for a structure that, when complete, looked very imposing among the fifteen or twenty picket, adobe, or stone houses surrounding it. The dignified name "The White House" soon became attached to the new hotel, possibly because it was the residence of the town's chief executive, or perhaps because of the color of its white boards, or, most probably, to honor Judge White, who was forced to take over its management in the absence of other proprietors.

Its construction was the first official act of the new leader of the colony. From the day of its completion, the life of the frontier community centered around it. In its beds slept at some time or another all the celebrities of the Panhandle, as well as the many cowboys who luxuriated in its hospitality as a change from the deadly routine of dugouts and a fare of beans and bacon. The cowboys, often having to come in over the great distances of the Panhandle, strangers in Clarendon, sometimes rode off again and left their unpaid bills to be settled, as was the custom, at a time in the future when it happened to suit their convenience or the convenience of the outfit for which they worked.

There was plenty of variety, excitement sometimes. When Goodnight and his wife stopped by, all normal activities ceased, for Goodnight demanded the best of everything and the services of all. When court was held, a tent city sprang up on the hotel grounds to make room for the many visitors. Prices were interesting: sugar was $60 a barrel; salt, $33; butter was 50¢ a pound; and the price of meals was correspondingly low.

In 1883 the hotel was leased to Mr. and Mrs. Phil- lips, a couple from Vernon, whose homestead section was bought three years later by the railroad for the sum of forty-eight hundred dollars, to be used as the town site for the new Clarendon that came into being with the coming of the railroad. After relinquishing their duties at the White House, Judge White and his wife moved to a home of their own on the property of Tom Morrison. Once across the threshold of this pleasant rock house, one found oneself as if by magic in another world, far removed from the prairie frontier. Behind the long porch outside lay the long room that served as a dining room and parlor. The furniture had been brought from the judge's mansion up north in Iowa. A grand piano stood in one corner; books lined the walls; on the dining table on occasion gleamed the finest silver and china. Around the big fireplace, in an atmosphere of kindliness and hospitality, the rough ways of many a discouraged settler were smoothed over by the graciousness of the Whites.

The tall and stately Lottie made a fitting wife for the judge, putting her culture and education, as did he, at the service of others. She liked people generally and was never happier than when entertaining a houseful of young folk with games and refreshments or when playing the tiny organ she had bought to make music for the Lord in the company of others so inclined.

CHAPTER 8

The Sign of Success

(The Quarter Circle Heart)

DURING the period that elapsed between Carhart's first invitation to White to head the colony and the latter's actually taking hold of affairs in Clarendon, the colony grew with the Panhandle and prospered far beyond the most optimistic expectations of its two founders, the minister Carhart and the New York banker Alfred Sully. Meanwhile the minister was transferred from Dallas to Fort Worth as a member of the quarterly conference, a position he retained for two years. By the time his term expired, both the church and his business affairs had reached a stage at which each demanded his undivided attention. A choice had to be made and in 1883 he asked to be released by the conference temporarily so that he might be entirely free from spiritual duties, at least for the next few years.

Colonists continued to pour in from everywhere. Cattle prices soared, and on all sides men grew rich overnight from herds fattened on free grass. The earliest outfits had been established by practical cowmen who had come to know the country well by traversing it each spring with their cattle drives headed north. Having learned from experience the benefits of the climate and range, they began one by one to settle more or less permanently on the rich grasslands of the Panhandle prairies and plains.

However, as the region continued to fulfill its promise and the cattle industry came to have a more stable basis, another kind of man came to encroach upon them: financiers, like John Adair, who neither knew nor desired to learn anything of the cattle business or the country but intended only to derive from both the fantastic profits offered by the combination of cattle, good grass, and the growing demand for beef. Occasionally one of these men fancied himself in the role of cattle king and so located in the Panhandle and set out to be a cattleman, but much more frequently the financiers had only one purpose: to organize a company that would derive its major profits not from stock raising but from the sale of shares to gullible persons far removed from the scene of interest.

As a result, many of the most important herds and brands, although established originally by individual Americans, eventually came into the hands of syndicates controlled to a great extent by foreign stockholders, usually British. In time these investments attracted numerous foreigners to the Panhandle. Unfortunately for them, many failed to adjust to the western frontier and, after a year or so, returned to the more familiar hedgerows of home. Among those who remained, the majority became valued citizens and contributed much to the development of the country and the foundations of its traditions.

Although considered peculiar and reserved people, they commanded respect for the reason that, even if odd, they were "usually damn good fellows who told the truth and could be depended on." Their chief difficulty lay in their misconception of the democratic standards of a region where all people were supposedly equal and every man worked. Even though they sometimes became legally naturalized, they were never fully able to understand or accept the true American ideal as exemplified by the cowboy who, when asked by a visiting aristocrat why everyone bore the title of "Mr." and "Mrs.," and if there were no leisure class, replied, "Sure, we've got lots of folks here that don't do anything, but we don't call 'em 'Lord' and 'Lady.' We just call 'em hoboes."

By 1880 the northwestern part of Texas was largely occupied and over its expanse grazed the hundreds of thousands of cattle which brought a great many men to affluence. As the history of the majority of the ranches identified with the period has already been presented many times over, only two of them will be given special notice here: the one because of the magnitude of its range, the other because its dramatic rise and fall were so typical of the era.

The XIT Ranch, although generally considered English because of the foreign capital used in its development, was principally owned and entirely operated by Americans. In 1882 Matheas Schoell was awarded against his one competitor the contract to build the capitol at Austin. For this undertaking he was to receive three million acres of land all in one block. Later, with the consent of the state, he assigned a three-fourths interest to a company composed of Abner Taylor, A. C. Babcock, John V. Farwell, and Charles B. Farwell. Out of this beginning grew the Capitol Syndicate. The original plan of the syndicate was to colonize the property, but upon the discovery that the Panhandle was not yet developed sufficiently for the success of a settlement project, the company established the ranch as a remunerative substitute—"to secure the land until the time of the farmer should come." As a result, the State of Texas acquired a structure second only to the Capitol at Washington and said to be among the seven largest buildings in the world, and the Panhandle acquired

one of the largest ranches in the United States with a range over two hundred miles in length.

Another huge ranch, the Diamond F outfit, had its beginning in 1883 when, through the efforts of B. B. Groom, the Francklyn Land and Cattle Company was organized. Six hundred and thirty-one thousand acres of land in Gray, Roberts, Hutchinson, Greer, and Carson counties were bought from the New York and Texas Land Company, which at the time controlled over five million acres of land acquired through the purchase of railroad scrip. The Diamond F holdings came later to be known as the White Deer Lands and as such played an important part in the settling of the country. Lord Rosebery, the son-in-law of Rothschild, and Francklyn, whose father-in-law owned most of the Cunard steamship line, were the principal stockholders.

Upon the establishment of the ranch, its promoter, B. B. Groom, and his son Harry became resident managers at respective salaries of ten and eight thousand dollars. Neither man knew anything about stock raising as pursued in the West and, furthermore, they had few practical ideas of any kind. The activities of the elder Groom not only brought disaster to the company but furnished amusement for the entire Panhandle. Tales are still told of the fine corrals and sheds built at Groom's headquarters on the plains, of specially ordered solid-copper branding irons that failed to imprint the diamond but marked the cattle with a big, rectangular scar instead, of shotguns that fired shells the size of a man's finger, of a remuda of horses with cropped ears, and of one fenced-in pasture that was twenty-eight miles wide and forty-two long.

Groom's first official act was to buy out the Cantrell brothers in order to remove them from White Deer Creek, and then, one by one, the other small operators whose herds were grazing within the range that soon was to pasture 80,000 head of cattle. The first big herd purchased was probably that of the Bar X outfit in Greer County.

Groom operated the enterprise with magnificent gestures. His expenditures during the few years of his regime are said to have run well into the millions of dollars. His outstanding characteristics, it seems, were an ability to convert others to his way of thinking and procedure and to spend with a lavish hand. At least, these were the attributes most influential on the affairs of the company, as the one brought about its existence in the beginning, and the other its untimely end.

The "Colonel," as Groom was called, was a pompous southern aristocrat with thoroughly un-American ideas about class distinctions—ideas that caused him no end of trouble, particularly when he attempted to treat cowboys in the same manner he had previously employed toward his black stableboys in Kentucky. One day, during a roundup, something happened to displease him, and with customary vehemence he gave vent to his wrath. The hand toward whom his remarks were directed sat calmly on his pony until the end of the tirade, then, without a word, climbed down, uncoiled his rope, and administered to the irate colonel the worst horsewhipping a man ever got. Groom, more humiliated than injured by the assault, demanded: "How dare you do such a thing to me? Don't you work for me?"

"Hell, no!" replied the still unruffled cowboy. "I'm an LX man."

This case of mistaken identity caused the manager of the Diamond F to notch the left ear of each of the outfit's four hundred fine horses, a procedure that doubtless gave them a ludicrous look, but enabled him to know when to speak his mind with impunity.

Dick Walsh, a Britisher who was at one time manager of the JA Ranch, claimed to have happened upon one of these animals years later, after he had returned to England to live. According to his story, the worst case of nostalgia he ever experienced came in the early morning hours when he chanced upon a London milk wagon pulled by a branded horse with a notched ear. Although the brand was indistinct, it was recognizable enough to revive vivid and happy memories of long-gone cowboy days in West Texas.

At the outset, Carhart, like many other newcomers to the West, had invested in a few hundred head of cattle, but his main concern had been the land and the colony, and he had paid little heed to his herd branded with a Quarter Circle Heart. In time, however, encouraged by the apparent success of the numerous large cattle companies, he and his partner, New York banker Alfred Sully, planned to extend operations by promoting through the banker's foreign connections an organization of sufficient capital to meet the demands of their ever-increasing ambitions. It was during this period that Sully paid his only visit to the colony. Having completed arrangements for the newly planned syndicate, he returned east to commence foreign negotiations, while Carhart set about materially to increase the size of the herd and other physical properties of the company.

Up until that time the competence of top hands like Alex Craig and Dave Wilson, together with the temporary management of Will Murdock, had sufficed to run the ranch, but with an enlarged outfit the addition of an experienced cowman as ranch manager became a necessity.

The Sign of Success 69

George Bradford, who had arrived on the scene with the first of the new cattle, a herd from down-state, was persuaded to assume charge temporarily; then some months later he was relieved by Al McKinney, whom Evans, owner of the Spade outfit, had suggested as the best man available for the job.

McKinney was a small, blond Irishman, twenty-five or thirty years old, wiry, quick-spoken, businesslike, a cowman who "knew his job and got it done." He scorned the characteristic boots and jingling spurs of his profession, but he had one personal vanity of which he was immensely proud: an impressive mustache that reached to the tips of his ears when properly waxed.

In a very few months after its conception a debenture company was organized and incorporated as planned, according to British law; after that, the minister sailed to England, to float the various kinds of stock of the company among prospective buyers there. In this manner he occupied himself during his first year away from the church.

By 1884 the 343 sections that made up his partnership holdings with Sully were leased for ninety-nine years to the new company in return for a consideration of $136,682, that lease in turn being surrendered to Sir Charles Clifford and John Eldon Gorst as trustees for the protection of the possessors of the many debentures that had been issued all over the British Isles. Cecil Kearney, gentleman of Middlesex County, was made secretary of the company.

Elated by his success and with high hopes for the future, Carhart returned to assume full responsibility as manager for the Clarendon Land Investment and Agency Company, as the new enterprise was known.

Early in the preceding year Frank Houston had purchased the Rockwall school grant, a block of about twenty thousand acres lying against the northwestern edge of the Heart range, and completely surrounding the Barton Ranch, which controlled much of McClellan Creek. Having bought out Barton, Frank Houston stocked his fertile range with a herd that he branded with a Bow and Arrow Cross.

Soon after his return from abroad, Carhart purchased Houston's entire holdings to convert them into a horse ranch for his outfit. An old English veterinarian named Archie Williams was put in charge. With the addition of this property, the Heart Ranch possessed three camps: one on McClellan Creek, one on Barton, and one at Brushy Springs. But as none of these was centrally located, a section two miles to the north of town on Carroll Creek was bought from another ex-minister, I. B. Carlich, and the dugout, which Carlich had gladly vacated in order to re-

turn to his home in Kansas, became the first company headquarters. Presently a two-room house, built partly of fieldstone and partly of sod, was put up to serve as the boys' bunkhouse.

When McKinney, the foreman, married, a comfortable frame house was made ready for the bride on an adjoining section. As the ranch office occupied its front room, it became the official headquarters and, as such, served as the home of any number of cowboys who later gained much prominence in the Panhandle.

By the time the lease was sold to the Clarendon Land Investment and Agency Company, the Heart range included several hundred thousand acres of land. In the center of this lay Clarendon. At any hour of the day cattle could be seen drifting along the town's crooked paths to water, undisturbed by the numerous freight wagons that rattled in and out as they came to load up with supplies for the various ranches located within trading distance of the busy little settlement.

CHAPTER 9

The Symbol of the West

(The Boy in the Boots and Stetson)

THE headquarters of most ranches, especially of those not occupied by the owner's family, was not as a rule a place of comfort but merely a point of departure and return. Often the only structures were a corral for the horses and a two-room ranch house, one room of which was large enough for the numerous bed rolls when unrolled, and the other for the kitchen stove, table, and chairs.

The outfit's personnel included a cook, a horse wrangler, and the necessary number of hands. The cook, although held in slight respect by the other men, was the most privileged character in the outfit and was allowed any insolence or indiscretion so long as he made good bread. The foundation of his popular "sour dough" was a yeast concoction kept in a well-guarded keg and made everlasting by constant replenishing with flour and water.

On the road the bread was cooked in a large black kettle —a Dutch oven—which stood on legs a little above the fire and was covered by a concave lid deep enough to hold a layer of coals, an arrangement that, with slow heat from both above and below, baked perfectly. Other than this, the fare consisted mainly of beans, potatoes, canned fruit as a special treat, and "sowbelly," that part of a hog so greatly appreciated by the laboring man because of its strength-sustaining qualities.

The cowboy, like the proverbial cobbler without shoes, got very little beef, and that little was most often supplied by some unlucky stray that happened across the outfits path. An unwritten law of the plains was never to eat the boss's cow. During range work the cook also drove the chuck wagon, a cumbersome affair covered by bows and a wagon sheet and drawn by four horses. Inside, protected from the elements, were the cowboys' bed rolls and provisions sufficient for several months.

In the beginning, when the country was unfenced, the cattle drifted badly, especially during the heavy snows and sleety winds of winter; by spring they were often scattered over a radius of a hundred and fifty miles or so. As soon as the weather broke, the business of rounding up the cattle over this large territory began.

In the absence of fenced pastures, the herds gathered

as the work progressed had to be held together at all times, which meant that besides riding fifteen or eighteen hours a day, a man had to stand his share of night guard as well. If there was a sufficient number of hands, the night shifts were divided into four, if not, three. A favorite, special horse was reserved for the work after sundown, since an animal that saw well in the dark and instinctively caught any unusual movements on the part of the cattle greatly facilitated for its rider the irksome duty of holding them at night. Singing, chewing, whistling—anything they had recourse to—was used to keep the eyes open after the day's many long hours in the saddle.

When all went well, the cattle bedded down quietly and everything was simple; but when circumstances out of the ordinary, such as a rain, thunder, or lightning, made them restless, they milled in fright and were restrained only with the greatest difficulty. At such times all hands were put on duty in an effort to prevent stampeding. When finally the cowboy's working day reached an end, he gratefully unrolled his bed on the nearest spot and crawled in to sleep like the dead, although sometimes tarantulas and rattlesnakes, without his knowing it, shared the warmth of his blankets until daylight.

In the early summer, after months of work in which all the ranch was covered, the wagons from the different ranches met for a general roundup. Fifty or sixty outfits would congregate, each with ten or fifteen men, to cut out and return to the home range their respective herds. When an owner was unable to be represented, some obliging cowboy took the absent man's cattle with his herd to drop them at their destination as he passed along the way.

After this came the branding and the separating of the cows and steers, then the midsummer trail drives to deliver the cattle already sold and the later, still longer drives to market in the fall.

As the drives often required months of steady travel, it was necessary that there be an abundance of water and grass for the cattle at all times on the way; consequently, the advantages of any trail were in proportion to the physical advantages of the country it traversed. The first step in preparing for a long drive was to ascertain the condition of the proposed route, with special emphasis on the amount of rainfall during the preceding months. After this was accomplished, the herd was gathered, the outfit hired, and all was in readiness to start.

The cattle numbered anywhere from a thousand to several thousand head, but a herd exceeding twenty-five hundred was rare, as it was unwieldy of movement and impossible to handle with advantage. The outfit was the same as that required for range work. Ten good cowboys

were able to handle any herd as a rule, but sometimes extra men were added.

At the beginning each man was given a certain position, which he retained during the entire drive. The chuck wagon took the lead, followed by the remuda, with the herd a mile or so in the rear, "pointers" at its head to keep the cattle following in the proper direction, men in the center to keep them lined up, and "drags" in the rear to push the sluggards up with the main body. As these last were prodded on, those in front automatically moved ahead. The chuck wagon stopped for noonday dinner, at a water hole when possible, thus breaking the day for the cattle as well as for the men by giving them time to slake their thirst and eat and rest; but if for any reason such a break was not advisable, the men ate by taking turns riding back to where the chuck wagon had stopped as the herd moved steadily on.

On the ideal day a distance of about fifteen miles was covered, with water available morning, noon, and night. It was considered necessary that a watering place be reached by dark, but sometimes the cattle were forced to go as long as two and even three days without drinking. When this was anticipated, the cattle were kept at the point of departure until midday, with ample time to get their fill before starting on the long, dry move; they were then driven far into the night and for as long a time as was required to enable them to reach water without fail before afternoon of the second day. During hot weather, after such a drive, it was necessary to put all hands to the front as the watering place was approached; otherwise, the thirst-crazed creatures exhausted themselves by running and often trampled down the weak ones among them as they rushed ahead to drink.

An intelligent driver, during a propitious season, could start out in the spring and, by the method of drifting instead of driving, always in the right direction, and never allowing an animal to take one single useless step, arrive in the fall at his destination with a herd that had gained material weight en route and was fattened and ready for market upon arrival. In trail driving, as in everything else, things of no apparent importance constituted the faint dividing line that separates success from failure. Remembering, for instance, that it is the habit of a cow always to walk aimlessly for a certain length of time before starting the day's grazing, the thoughtful driver made sure that his cattle were headed in the right direction immediately upon arising from their night's bedding ground; in this way and with little effort, several miles of territory were covered during those hours set apart for feeding, long before the real journey of the day began.

When the end of the trail was finally reached and the cattle were delivered at their proper destination, the men, grimy and travel-worn after months on the range, released from their days of labor and loneliness, would rush in a body to the nearest eating house to devour unbelievable quantities of french-fried potatoes and the best and biggest steaks on the menu; then, having satisfied that physical need, they would move on to the nearest saloon to seek relaxation in gambling and drinking.

By early winter, line camps were established and each morning two riders started out in opposite directions to meet two men from the adjoining camps, thus forming a complete human fence around the ranch. Often a tent or covered wagon was the cowboy's only protection against the bitter weather. Sometimes, however, a convenient hill offered a welcome chance to "dig in" for the winter.

The cowboy's dugout,[1] unlike the larger and more permanent ones on the Carroll, was simply a warm and protected refuge in which to spend an occasional night. Whatever its purpose, however, a dugout was always located on the bank of a creek or ravine, at an elevation safe above the flood level of rising waters. The logs and branches that formed the base of the roof were slanted slightly toward the front to facilitate drainage, and a run-off was dug from the door down to the creek. If the camp was to be used frequently, a door made of poles and grass and chinked with mud was added and sometimes even a stone fireplace. In such crude dwellings the cowboys lived through the long, lonely winter months. They slept from eight at night until four in the morning, then got up to begin their riding; they returned to camp in mid-afternoon, to talk—the two of them, for they usually stayed in pairs—until weariness drove them to their early bed. Day after day, this was their existence, with only an occasional holiday in town, where gambling and drinking quickly wiped out the savings of the previous months' work.

At the beginning of the season, each cowboy received

[1] See Everett Dick, *The Sod-House Frontier, 1854–1890*, p. 110, for a more detailed description of the dugout.

an allotment of eight or ten horses; these made up his mount and were his exclusively as long as he worked. Everyone was forced to do his share of the "busting," as there were always forty or more broncs to be "broken" in the spring, with some of the old mean ones to be broken all over again after each winter's idleness. The system was to climb on and stay on, if one could, praying that if a fall did come, the landing would be made in the soft sand and not on a stony hill or among the thorns of a cactus plant.

The horses were of old Spanish stock from Mexico and South Texas and were a breed far superior to those of today, which have acquired, through the addition of racing and saddle blood, a finer appearance but, for the same reason, have lost much of their former intelligence. A good cowpony must be active, quick-witted, and bridle-wise, like the polo pony, but it must possess besides an instinctive ability to follow a cow from the herd after only one showing and without the help even of the rider's directing reins.

The old-time saddle was a clumsy affair called a "still tree." Its iron fork formed the horn to which the rope was attached, but its horsehair pockets served little purpose other than that of adornment. Their irritating slap against the horse's flanks as he moved not only frightened the cattle during the roundup but terrified the recently broken broncs and added materially to their misbehavior when first ridden. Unlike the Mexican saddle, the stirrups were not equipped with *tapaderos* (leather shields to prevent the foot from slipping through).

The cowboy's way of riding was and still is the same as the Indian's, being merely an adjustment to the motion of the horse through complete bodily relaxation. So perfectly are the movements of man and horse coordinated that they appear as one when in action. There is no more thrilling sight than that of a good cowboy and a well-trained pony as with swaying grace they move at full speed across the prairie in pursuit of a recalcitrant cow.

By today's standards, the cowboy's wages were very small except in the case of "fighting men" who, because of their propensity for quick and straight shooting, were hired at double the usual wages and even more when the need arose. People in those days were not so concerned over money, and the monthly recompense was often of little importance, as proved by the attitude of the cowboy who, when told by his employer as they stood together by the bar that he was to receive a ten-dollar raise, considered the announcement, then with a sigh of resignation replied, "All right, but here I am having a hell of a time drinking up last month's thirty dollars, and when it gets to forty, I'm dead sure it'll damn near kill me."

The cowboy wore a fantastic outfit composed of boots made by Corbett, Naum, or McLaughlin, checkered trousers called "California doe-skins," a bright shirt, and a bright kerchief that not only added color to the general effect but proved useful when pulled across the mouth and nose against dust. Fancy gauntlets and a white Stetson completed the costume so unsuited in its flamboyance to the stern and rugged background of which it was a part.

Those were the days when people expected to work for a living, and big pay and short hours were unknown, when the labor was heavy and the fare was plain—and life was truly hard but rich. As one old-timer expressed it, "even if it was tough and lonely, there was something about the feel of a good horse under you or the excitement of a milling herd or the thrill that came over you when you were standing guard alone in a storm, watching the lightning play on the cattle's horns, that got you. And if you happened to like that kind of life, you never found anything else to take its place."[2]

[2] William C. (Buster) Culdwell, cowboy on the RO Ranch, in an interview with the author (undated transcript in the Lewis Papers, Archives, Dallas Historical Society).

In order that the reader may fully understand the cowboy of long, long ago—that splendid fellow who was the prototype of the fictional figure of today—it is necessary, before attempting to tell exactly what he was and what he stood for, to tell what he was not.

To begin with, he was not of the same species as the contemporary hand who retains few of the old-time cowboy's sterling qualities, although to all outward appearances he is unchanged—walking with the same awkward, stiff-legged gait that comes from booted heels, bowed legs, and overmuch time in the saddle, wearing pants that threaten momentarily to slip from hips too slender to restrain them, and speaking, if he speaks at all, in the hesitant, drawling lingo of the plains. The old-timer quite simply was not just any man who made his living by working with cattle; nor was he the sort of cowboy who drifted from outfit to outfit, contributing little besides his daily labor to the life around him and asking only a faithful pony in return; nor was he the cattle king who, with slight effort, was swept to fabulous success on the rising tide of the era. He was, instead, the man in whose heart lay a deep and lasting love of the land, one who looked on his job as a means to an end and, having found the job itself to his liking, continued in it—gradually and often enough,

as he worked, developing himself into a man of property and the frontier range into the land of his desire.

He was a composite of many types from many places. There were hunters, soldiers, merchants; boys from down south who had tired of cotton fields in the sun; steady plodders from up north who sought the easy wealth of the West; gentlemen from the South who had fled the havoc wrought by the war; Britishers from titled families—second sons forced out of the fold by the law of entailment—such as the nephews of Cardinal Vaughan and Lord Beresford, and even one who claimed—rather convincingly, too—that he was the son of the king of England; men who retained to the end the ideals of the gentle homes from which they came and the sense of responsibility and the conduct imposed on them by the code of their aristocratic origin. Forced by the exigencies of their adopted life to acquire the ruder virtues necessary for survival on the frontier, these scions of great families blended the sturdy worth of the pioneer with the traditions of a higher civilization, and from this combination of the new world and the old created a matchless specimen of mankind.

The region into which these men of varied backgrounds who became that uniquely American figure, the cowboy, had immigrated was an isolated virgin country where life was unhampered by the compulsions of religion, custom, or the often unfair standards of sophisticated society. As it was impossible to live other than simply, family prestige and power of wealth counted for little. In the absence of such external props and disguises, the true inner being was easily recognizable. Consequently, a man was what his behavior showed, and each man was the equal of the other until he proved himself otherwise.

There was no law and no established order; only the needs of the community determined its ethics. Of necessity, life was cooperative. Danger was on all sides; a new world was in the making with much to be accomplished. As the large cattle outfits expanded, a system resembling that of feudal England arose, wherein an employer's rights and property were something to be protected to the death. The land offered its rewards to all alike, with a certain amount of success assured any individual who expended intelligent effort. Thus, the struggle for existence was not a conflict of man against man, such as prevails in a more highly organized industrial society, but an endless battle with the hazards of the environment—mostly the weather. Failure was, as a rule, the result of personal inertia and, because of that, was not accompanied by the bitterness of spirit or sense of frustration usual where competition between man and his fellow is keen.

In his long and lonely years on the range, the cowboy reacted to his surroundings much in the manner of the primitive men who had occupied the land before him. Each day he watched the sun rise in the east, then sink that night below the western horizon. He was conscious of the benefits of Mother Earth's lavish gifts and the devastation wrought by her withdrawal of them. Through close association with nature, he learned his proper relation to the general scheme of the universe and a graceful acceptance of matters beyond his control. His religion was a form of pantheism, centering entirely on the practical needs of the present and having no connection with either his ethics or the rewards of a future life.

His destiny lay largely in his own hands. To the past he paid little heed. The future to a great extent he himself determined. The qualities he respected most were willingness to work, honesty, fair play, fearlessness, and loyalty both to man and to the land that gave him his chance. Such was the cowboy of old, a beautiful example of the American ideal of individual enterprise and democratic regard for the rights of man.

CHAPTER 10

The Frontier Merchant

(*A One-Man Chamber of Commerce*)

IN the same year that Lewis Henry Carhart withdrew temporarily from his church there came to reside in Clarendon a young man who, through his presence there, created a situation unique in the history of the Panhandle. In spite of the prejudice against his race, this plump, curly-haired little Jew, Morris Rosenfield by name, came to occupy a position of influence exceeded only by that of Judge White, and to contribute as much as, if not more than, any other man toward the growth of a colony founded by gentiles for the promotion of a Christian faith.

Long before the arrival of the Jewish merchant, as far back as 1849, a bluff overlooking the head of the Trinity River had been chosen by Major Ripley Arnold and his dragoons as the most strategic point from which to stretch their cordon of protecting military posts across the edge of the Texas frontier. During the soldiers' four years of occupancy, there arose around them a settlement that came in time to be called Fort Worth, after their cantonment, Camp Worth. By the early 1870's the little town had grown into the commercial center of a new West. Like Dodge City to the north, which had opened the Panhandle to settlers at the beginning, Fort Worth was destined to become a gateway through which they would pass as they moved on to the West.

In general, American centers of population and commerce have arisen at places indicated as advantageous by the direction of the nation's waterways. In the Panhandle, however, it was commonly believed that the rivers, even those which emerge as navigable streams farther down state, followed an underground course, hidden beneath wide and sandy arroyos, appearing as little more than trickling streams, except as the result of occasional head-water rises. This theory caused the towns to be situated along artificial instead of more natural routes, and the coming of the railroad thus became an issue of utmost importance, as with bands of steel it welded settlements into permanent position, marked infallible signposts for commerce, and tied the outlying districts to the salient points already established.

Fort Worth was from the beginning a railroad center. Among its citizens were men of enterprise and foresight who realized that theirs was the responsibility and to them would accrue much of the advantage of opening to the world the country to the north and west. Consequently, in September, 1873, a mass meeting was called for the purpose of forming an organization to construct a railroad across the uninhabited area. A charter was obtained requiring the completion of twenty-five miles of roadbed within three years from the passage of the act, and thirty more each two years thereafter.

At once an engineering corps began the location of the line, which, when completed many years later, connected the Gulf of Mexico with the northern states and infused with its lifeblood of progress the plains of Texas. The initial plan was to build only to the Canadian River and there to connect with the Denver and New Orleans railroad, thus forming a through line that would serve the ranching interests already in existence and act as a stimulus to future agricultural development. According to the terms of the charter, the line should have been completed within ten years or less, but the panic that followed close upon its inception stopped its progress at once, and it was not until November 27, 1881, that actual laying of the rails commenced.

During this period Fort Worth continued to look toward the northwest for its own development, and the neighboring city of Dallas watched with jealous interest the potential for commerce that lay along the proposed line of track. As one settlement after another sprang into existence, Sanger Bros., Dallas's oldest mercantile firm, undertook a policy of expansion through supplying stock on easy terms to any worthy merchant who dared precede the railroad onto the frontier.

One day in 1882 Rosenfield, who at the time was employed as a sort of "general man" around the store, was summoned to the office. When he walked in on that particular Monday morning, he saw awaiting him all the executives of both the retail and wholesale branches of the firm—Alex Sanger, Phillip Sanger, W. O. Connor, Tom Barry, and Seymour Meyer. Alex Sanger was the first to speak.

"Morris," he said, "You have been chosen from 265 employees to help us out of a difficulty. We have been forced to take over a bankrupt stock valued at about eighty-five thousand dollars, which stock, we feel, under proper management, can easily be converted into the cash necessary to reimburse us without loss. A town called Clarendon has been started up in the Panhandle country. Our plan is for you to proceed there, open up for business, and dispose of this merchandise to advantage. What do you think of the idea?"

Carhart was well known in Dallas,[1] and Morris, like the other businessmen in town, had heard often of the minister's operations at Clarendon and was more than eager to accept an opportunity to look over the new West.

With Rosenfield's decision to establish himself in Clarendon, another stone of stability was laid in the economic foundation of the southern part of the Panhandle. The merchants preceding him had been itinerant adventurers whose business activities were only temporary expedients at best. Morris was not one of these. He was a trained mercantile man in the employ of an established firm.

Soon all preliminary arrangements were complete. Tom Barry, a drummer in the employ of Sanger and familiar with the territory, was delegated to act as guide and assistant in locating the store. As the railroad went no farther than Wichita Falls, all freight had to be hauled from that point by wagon at a cost of $2.25 per hundred pounds. Having given the freighters a few days' head

start, the two men proceeded to the end of the line in readiness for their overland trip of 180 miles, the remaining distance to their destination on the Salt Fork.

From Wichita Falls they set out in a glistening new Concord hack drawn by four young and spirited Spanish mules, a propitious beginning that did not last the journey; vehicle and teams were changed from time to time and both deteriorated materially with each successive stop on the way west. When they finally reached the last hill before Clarendon, the ascent was accomplished only through the combined efforts of all the passengers, who alighted to push from behind the dilapidated coach in which they traveled and to urge from the front the even more worn-out mules that pulled it.

Among the travelers were a state senator and a representative on their way to look over the region they had recently been elected to represent and a black soldier, dressed in uniform and armed to the hilt, bound for Fort Elliott after a sojourn of some months in the penitentiary as a result of having failed in line of duty during the hold-up of a train on which he happened to be traveling. (Although it is an army rule that a man must fight whenever or wherever the occasion demands if he be present in uniform, this soldier wisely considered cowardice the better part of valor when facing masked bandits and chose to

---

[1] It is highly probable that Carhart's financial arrangements were made with the Texas Land and Mortgage Company. That company was composed largely (perhaps entirely) of English stockholders and had as its Dallas manager a man named Wellesley. Rumor was that Wellesley was the unacknowledged grandson of the Duke of Wellington, but the author has found nothing to substantiate that rumor.

risk imprisonment rather than the death that would have been certain had he offered resistance to the robbers.) He was put to ride on top of the hack with the driver in the wind and heat while the politicians and the Sanger representatives occupied the more comfortable seats inside.

They had settled for their long journey from Wichita Falls when the hotel door slammed behind another soldier as he dashed out to join the party—a handsome young captain on his way from Washington to take charge of the infirmary at the fort. In answer to his polite inquiry as to his seat, the stage driver, a rough old fellow, pointed inside and said, "Don't ask me; ask them already in there."

It so happened that Tom Barry, as a boy, had seen several years of service in the Confederate army and still held without modification the opinions bred by the mixed emotions of war and youth. Despite the intervening years, he continued to find a Yankee decidedly distasteful and so spoke up saying, "I hope you understand, sir, that I, for one, refuse to ride anywhere with a blue-coat."

Without replying to this rude welcome, the officer climbed on top to take a place beside the black private. After twenty-five miles, a shady creek was reached, and the first stop was made. While the animals were being fed and watered, the passengers both inside and out alighted to stretch their legs on the prairie and to eat in picnic style the lunch they carried along in boxes. The first thing the army captain did, on getting down from his perch, was to pull from his pocket a bottle of excellent whiskey which he proceeded courteously to pass around as if nothing of an unpleasant nature had occurred.

The morning had been long and hot and tiring, so, although his convictions remained unchanged, Barry's dislike of a "blue-coat" was not, at that point, equal to his thirst. Eagerly he accepted the proffered drink, which was followed by a second, then a third, and so on.

Long before the supply ran low, the "enemy" had mellowed into a friendly state of inebriation in which all differences of opinion were lost, and, by the time Clarendon was reached, the South had capitulated so completely to the North that the chief antagonist had forgotten entirely the real purpose of his trip. Having disposed of his end of the business by the simple gesture of transferring it to Rosenfield, Barry traveled straight on to Mobeetie to spend a hilarious vacation in the company of his new Yankee friend and the other officers awaiting them there.

Rosenfield was now alone and in full charge. On looking around, he was pleased to find a situation most favorable to his plans. The business section of Clarendon, which extended down one side of a single, long block, included only one general store, a small branch shop where

Major Van Horn retailed at a profit of 300 percent the more or less discarded remnants of his sutler's stock from Fort Elliott. The new merchant saw that this competitor could easily and quickly be eliminated by a policy of underselling. Therefore, as soon as he had located his store in the only available place, a building previously used by Carhart for storage, he began to advertise, with special emphasis on the modern style of his merchandise and the low prices at which it was being offered. On the opening day, every man, woman, and child in town and every cowboy who could find time to ride the distance from his ranch purchased at least one article from the varied assortment. From then on customers were never lacking and trade was fine.

Contrary to the usual commercial problem, the only difficulty was not one of demand but of supply. Rosenfield was able to sell anything, once he had it, but his requests for new merchandise were answered very unsatisfactorily. All shipments were delayed in delivery, and many failed to arrive at all. One day, in a fit of impatience, he wrote to the Sangers telling them that because the inhabitants of the community and its surrounding district had learned to depend on him for everything they used, it was a matter of pride as well as profit that their wants be supplied; that

unless the home office could fill his orders more promptly, he was ready to resign.

A chief cause of the delayed deliveries may have been lack of interest. The bankrupt stock originally consisted of ranch equipment, groceries, wearing apparel—everything, Rosenfield often said, except a church pulpit, and he never knew why that was wanting in a district where preaching was the avocation of the major portion of the population. The Sangers' intention was never to operate permanently but only as long as necessary to rid themselves of a conglomerate mixture of overstock.

At this time Max Rosenfield was the firm's head credit man. Having heard of his brother's letter, he wrote hastily to Clarendon to tell Morris that, knowing the policy of their firm, he felt certain that what remained of the bankrupt stock could be bought as a whole for sixty cents on the dollar. If trade was as good as reported he would suggest that the Clarendon representative raise the necessary capital, buy it in, and go into business for himself.

During Morris's two years in the West, he and Judge White had become warm friends, so he hastened to the lawyer to lay the matter before him and to ask his advice. Fortunately for the merchant, the judge had recently inherited a few thousand dollars that were still uninvested. Although not a businessman, he was quick to recognize the possibilities of a big store in Clarendon, particularly one run by someone as honest and capable as Morris. As a result, a partnership was formed in which Judge White was to contribute the capital, Rosenfield the experience and personal attention. As Rosenfield felt it better, for racial reasons, not to use his name, the new firm was called B. H. White and Company. Meanwhile, Major Van Horn, who owned the only other general store, had become discouraged and was ready to depart. It was in the building he had occupied that the new firm opened.

Business in those days was conducted on a basis very different from that of today. The integrity of the individual, not the collateral behind the debt, was the paramount issue. For instance, at the time the stock changed hands, there were some $18,000 in outstanding accounts on the books. Tom Barry, who returned to complete negotiations for Sanger, on inquiring as to the cash value of the book accounts, was told "dollar for dollar."

"Maybe you're right, Rosie," he said, "but they surely do not appear that way to me. Who, for instance, is this fellow Dempsey Forrest who is down for two thousand dollars?"

"He's a catcher of wild horses."

"What does he have to secure this debt?"

"A few mustangs," answered the merchant. "Some rope, and a lot of honor. I don't need anything else."

Because business had to be conducted along such uncertain lines or not at all, Rosenfield had learned to appraise a man's character at a glance. His judgment was rarely wrong, as the following incident proves. One day he lent ten dollars to a man whose name even was unknown to him. Months later, an acquaintance from miles away was in town for court. On seeing the merchant, he stopped him, greeted him, and said, "By the way, I have ten dollars for you. Last week some fellow I didn't know came into my store and gave it to me. He told me he had borrowed it from a fellow *he* didn't know and who the fellow was I didn't know from his description, but we knew I'd run across him sometime. And now that I see you, I guess you must be the one, so here it is."

As many of the cowboys were drifters, the ranch for which each worked "stood" for his debts. Their separate accounts, listed each under its own heading, together with the general ranch bills for groceries, equipment, and so forth, were mailed out as one single statement at the end of the month. The whole amount often aggregated a sum of several thousands of dollars, the list of items covered innumerable sheets of paper, and a system of bookkeeping was required that kept Jim Otey and J. J. Staunton busy from early morning until late at night.

There was little currency in circulation, and checks, acceptable for any amount—even less than a dollar—were the usual means of exchange. The stubs were invaluable in straightening out the personal accounts between ranch hand and employer at the time of adjustment. When some unexpected occurrence made cash necessary, a transient gambler was sought out—any one of the many who came up from Fort Worth periodically to relieve the cowboys of their earnings. After having located one, the merchant would say, "I need some money quickly. Do you have any?"

"Sure, I've got plenty. How much do you want?"

"About five hundred dollars. Shall I give you a due bill for it?"

"Don't bother. Just hand it back to me whenever it's convenient."

The nearest bank was at Harrold, a distance of many miles. The suggestion was often made that the firm open a banking branch, but Judge White refused on the ethical as well as legal grounds that he and his partner did not have the capital necessary to guarantee the deposit. Consequently, the checks and money that often remained in the safe were kept there purely as a convenience to the store's customers. Sometimes as much as sixty thousand dollars in paper currency was on hand, placed there by trusting depositors who had only the merchant's verbal assurance that it would be kept intact until needed.

All merchandise was freighted in from Wichita Falls, either by small outfits of two or three wagons or by larger bulltrains in which there were as many as fifteen or twenty wagons. Each wagon was pulled by six or eight oxen or mules, and the driver held the reins as he walked alongside, cracking a long bullwhip, or rode in his saddle astride one of the lead animals. These outfits traveled by schedule, never making more than twenty-five miles a day as a protection to the teams. Having been notified of the time of departure, the merchant could calculate almost exactly the location of the train during any part of the journey.

Bill Ross, the company's first freighter, held the job until the coming of barbed wire, when he took up fencing, a new and more profitable line of work. Then, with his employer's assistance, he agreed with the Francklyn Land and Cattle Company upon a contract which in the few years of its duration remunerated him so highly that he moved on to Hereford to become one of the town's wealthiest and most influential citizens.

Bill's honesty was above reproach, and, like the other old-timers, he deemed a man's word as good as his bond. He started working for the Francklyn Land Company immediately after it had gone into the hands of the receiver and Groom had been replaced as manager by George Tyng, a New England Yankee whose business methods were as meticulous as Bill's were careless. Much to Bill's disgust and contrary to the custom of the West, the contract was not an oral one but a written and signed agreement that described in detail every posthole, nail, or yard of barbed wire to be used and covered countless pages.

Toward the completion of the work, by which time Bill had already begun to realize the magnitude of his profits, he stepped into the store one day to visit with his former employer. During the ensuing conversation, he reached into his pocket and, having drawn out the voluminous papers on which the contract was written, pointed to it and remarked dryly, "If Tyng's pencil had been just a trifle longer, he would have made me a millionaire sure enough, now wouldn't he?"

The other freighter was James Kilfoil, one of the many buffalo hunters who later made fortunes by collecting the bones of the millions of animals slaughtered during the early years. The custom was to gather, in passing, the many bones scattered around on the prairies, then

to deposit them in a pile designated as private property by a stake inscribed with the owner's initials. These skeleton pyramids rose sometimes to a height of thirty feet before being razed as they were made ready for delivery to the freight cars that awaited them on the railroad tracks in Wichita Falls.

The market price for the bones was good, as they were in great demand by the manufacturers of glue, buttons, and fertilizer, and much preferred to cattle bones. Lucrative as this business was, however, it was usually carried on only in conjunction with something else, most often freighting. Kilfoil's routine was to make the trip up loaded with merchandise for Clarendon, then on his return to fill his otherwise empty wagons with the bones that lay at convenient places on the trail.

During the days of its prosperity, the store served many purposes other than mercantile. Below its long main room was a 150-foot cellar in which was stored, together with the company's drygoods, the liquor secretly owned by the hard-drinking inhabitants of a strictly prohibition town. Because of his leniency in the matter, Rosenfield was a general favorite with the whiskey drummers and Mobeetie saloonkeepers who packed the back of his buckboard with the choicest of intoxicating beverages whenever he passed through town.

As firearms were also taboo and it was a general custom in the West to go heavily armed, some provision had to be made for the weapons of the visitors in town. Upon the long counter reserved for their disposal at the back the six-shooters sometimes grew into so large a pile as to give the room the appearance of a miniature armory.

The store also served as a general meeting place in the absence of the more usual form of amusement house—the saloon and gambling hall. All kinds of games of chance were very popular. By offering as a prize some article too costly for the average cowboy's purse, the canny merchant was able to please his customers and to increase his own profits. The winner was decided in various ways: when the contestants were all experienced gamblers, by a few rounds of poker or dice-throwing; otherwise, by the simpler method of pitching silver dollars at a wide crack in the floor. The storeowners were the only participants who never lost, since, in any case, the "kitty" or the carefully aimed dollars landed eventually in their cash register.

But Rosenfield possessed many admirable qualities other than his shrewdness as a businessman. He had a most friendly, sympathetic nature and a keen desire to assist in the development of the country. He had wonderful powers of mimicry and a beautiful tenor voice, both of which he shared at any time for any purpose. For years he was soloist in the Methodist choir without any remuneration whatsoever other than his personal pleasure in the advancement of a cause he considered worthy even though connected with a creed so opposed to his own. Through his many lines of contact with people, he became so involved in the affairs of each one individually that, like the banker of today, he exerted a wide influence on the collective life of the colony.

During his first years of residence in Clarendon, Morris lived alone in a small room at the back of his store.

But in May, 1884, the same year in which he and Judge White bought out the interests of Sanger Bros., he married Regina Goldberg, a cousin from Germany, and built his own house up near the ridge. Although far removed from her native land and never able to master the English language, his wife was happy in her new home, content with being a good mother, the town's best cook, and wife to her "Rosie," as everyone affectionately called the Panhandle's leading pioneer merchant and one-man Chamber of Commerce.

CHAPTER II

The Ways of Democracy

(None to Serve Them)

THOUGH difficult in the extreme, life on the frontier presented an inviting as well as an austere side. Its hardships, being chiefly physical, were far more easily borne than the spiritual conflicts of existence today. Especially was this true of the women, except in rare cases where fear and loneliness had disastrous effects on their emotional balance. Children needed little supervision. When turned loose upon the prairie, they simply grew. Houses were small and scantily furnished, and the men knew how to do the homely chores, like cooking and washing, as well as the female folk did. When illness or other circumstances disrupted a wife's routine, her mate proved a willing and capable substitute. And this was fortunate for all concerned, as servants were an unheard-of luxury. Some few families annexed an orphan or a poor relative who did the drudgery for her keep, and one or two managed to acquire for a time some trained domestic who had drifted in from the fort. There were not many blacks, although a few of the ranches employed them as cooks and several lived in the colony.

"Old Harrison," who was man-of-all-work around the White House, had among other duties the pleasant job of supplying the hotel table with wild game. He could be seen almost any sunny morning with his gun across his shoulder, headed toward one of the numerous bunches of antelope that grazed constantly around the edge of town.

Billy Freeman, too, worked now and then at the hotel but, because of previous experience as a jockey, spent most of his time breaking broncs for the Heart outfit. His brother, Prince, worked for Mrs. Parks. Both were excellent cooks and were so sought after by the female members of the population that arguments over them sometimes grew serious.

Then there was Martha, who had known Mrs. Goodnight during the days when both lived within the shadow of a frontier fort. While very young she had been taken as a slave into the family of Dennis Murphy to act as nurse for his four children. By the time he moved from Jacksboro to the Panhandle to join his friend Goodnight, the little boys had grown into men, the girls had finished

their education in the East and were settled married women, and Martha herself was a mother.

She and her three children, Hattie, Maud, nicknamed "Seat," and Tom, nicknamed "Man," traveled in the same wagon with Mrs. Murphy on the long ride west. Charlie, the older Murphy boy, was in charge of the cattle herd; Will drove the wagon in which the women rode; and the father set the trail in the freight wagon loaded with their household goods. On reaching the JA headquarters, the family moved in with the Goodnights in the big house and Martha and her brood occupied a room at the back. She was the cook, and Mrs. Murphy was the housekeeper, but at times when the work piled up, the mistress of the ranch also lent a hand.

Behind the main house rose a hill, a pretty background for the group of buildings nestled at its base. Leading to these was the long lane that divided the buffalo pasture from the sorghum field. Soon every person in the country was a friend of Martha and her children, especially "Seat" and "Man," who were a familiar sight swinging on the main gate as they waited to open it for any generous guest who chanced through.

Those were happy days for the black children. In the other main house lived a relative of Goodnight's, Henry Taylor, and his three boys, Crockett, Walter, and June.

Crockett and the black girl, Hattie, were about the same age, and they were the leaders of the mixed band of children of which Crockett was everyone's favorite.

All the ranch fences were of cedar posts and wire except the one around the headquarters, on the broad plank rail of which hung the cowboys' saddles when not in use. The children thought it great sport to climb into these and pretend to be riding in pursuit of retreating Indians, or to sneak into the corral to play, when the boss's back was turned, until they were discovered and chased out by a threatening crack from one of the freighter's long "black-snakes" that hung on the wall. Sometimes they timorously followed Crockett as he dashed across the pasture in full view of the buffalo grazing there, or crept away from busy parents in the early morning to spend the day robbing birds' nests and hunting baby rabbits. On Sundays they were made to dress and sit quietly while Mrs. Goodnight read aloud stories from the Bible, and at Christmas the gifts for Martha's children hung on the tree with those of the family. Until she was white-haired, "Seat" kept carefully packed away in the bottom of a trunk the broken pieces of the china doll that was Santa's gift to her that first holiday at the JA Ranch.

The following summer the Murphys moved to a log house many miles away, from which Dennis rode the line for Goodnight. There Martha and her youngsters lived in a lean-to of pickets and adobe attached to the back of the house.

Martha and her son, Tom, slept in the only bed and the two little girls lay on a pallet beside them on the dirt floor. Sometimes rats came through a hole in the wall to nibble at the ears of the sleepers, and once a rattler crawled from under the feather "tick" that lay piled on top of the other mattresses to protect the little ones against lightning.

After the move, the children, like the grown-ups, had scant time for play. Even the smaller ones worked in the fields, following down the rows behind their master, to scatter, as they went, the grain seeds that hung in small sacks around their necks, or struggling to "strip out" the Johnson grass that even in the new country was the farmer's foe.

Martha and Mrs. Murphy toiled side by side from early dawn until after dark. There were twenty-five cows to be milked each day, guineas, ducks, and chickens to be fed, and churning to be done. In the big garden crowder peas, butterbeans, red beans, and black-eyed peas were grown which would be dried for winter use.

The cooking was a small job, since people then did not require such varieties of food as now. If cabbage was served, it was prepared in quantity to make the main dish and was accompanied by little besides cornbread and buttermilk. But the sewing took much time and was hard and tedious. The usual form of dress of the women in the country was the "Mother Hubbard" which, like all feminine apparel, could, if desired, be adorned by yokes and tucks and ruffles. It was worn over petticoats that were full of lace and very difficult to sew. These were starched before wearing until they rattled like newspapers in the wind.

At the end of day, when supper was over and the red-checkered tablecloth had been brushed clean of crumbs, the grown-ups seated themselves around the big stone fireplace with Mrs. Murphy dozing at one side and Martha sewing or mending at the other. While the children played quietly on the floor in a corner, Mr. Murphy read aloud from newspapers many months old or told and retold the stories of his experiences on the trail or of his niece who was stolen by the Indians and never found. In the firelight's cheery glow, labors of the day were forgotten in the simple pleasures of a frontier home.

Far away to the north of them lived Birl Brown, who early in life had been drafted into service as "nursemaid" for the fast-arriving Koogle babies. His presence in the Panhandle was the result of his having been kidnapped by a trail driver.

At the time the black boy was stolen, his home was in Tyler, and he was living out from town in a "rent house" owned by the man in whose canning factory his mother worked. One day, with some other children, he had wandered farther than usual from home and was playing at the side of a road out beyond town when a trail herd happened by. Milk cows were the only kind familiar to the youngsters, so in curiosity they followed along behind the moving cattle, amazed at the sight of so many hundreds of funny-looking long-horned animals all together.

As they scampered around the edge of the herd, a man on horseback rode up and, having stopped, inquired if any one of them wanted to take a ride. He was a pleasant-looking fellow who spoke in a kindly tone, so they were not frightened but, with natural reticence, they were slow to respond to this unusual overture. The stranger turned to Birl and, speaking directly to him, said, "I know this boy would like a ride. Now wouldn't you?"

The flattery of having thus been singled out, as well as a boy's delight at the prospect, prompted a quick "Yes, sir."

"Very well," the man answered. "Somebody will be

along in a minute. I'll wait here with you and see for sure that you get that ride."

Soon a wagon pulled by a team of oxen lumbered around the bend of the road. The driver, Birl later learned, was the outfit's cook. After a short, mumbled conversation between the two men, the one on horseback leaned down, picked the boy up, and placed him at the black driver's side on the wagon seat, at the same time instructing the driver to guard well the new passenger and to buy him candy and apples as soon as a store was reached. Having tossed into his lap the coins necessary for the purchase, he galloped off and was soon out of sight in front of the herd.

For a long time Birl was too engrossed to realize what was happening. This stranger was as kind and friendly as the other man had been; fruit and sweetmeats were luxuries to which the boy was unaccustomed; and besides, there was the thrill of actually riding along behind all those strange cattle. But by sundown he had grown tired, and the pleasure of this new experience began to pall. Having decided at last that he had ridden far enough, he gathered courage to ask the driver timidly if he would please take him home, a request which was quickly dismissed by the suggestion that he be a good boy and he would get back to his mother soon enough.

His fears thus temporarily allayed, Birl settled down again to chat with his older companion and to watch the sights along the road. Soon another town was reached and passed, and the wagon was leaving its outskirts when a bunch of goats appeared across their path. Boze (that was the cook's name) wasted no time investigating the reason for their presence there but pulled the team to a sudden halt, drew out his gun, and shot one of the goats, and then, after having climbed down and dressed his slaughter, threw it behind, remounted, and drove on as if the procedure were all a part of the day's routine.

During the hour or more consumed by this interruption, Birl's excitement over so unusual an experience prevented thoughts of a more serious nature, but, when the journey was resumed and night drew nearer, his unhappiness returned, and he began once more to beg to be taken home. Upon the realization that his insistent pleadings were of no avail and that the driver did not intend to turn around, the boy ceased all efforts at self-control and gave way to a burst of tears that Boze, in his clumsy way, tried to soothe. But the sobs grew harder and continued on until in desperation the man took from his pocket a bottle, the contents of which he forced by main strength down the throat of the weeping child.

When Birl awakened from his drunken stupor many,

many hours later, it was well into the morning of the next day. Wagon and herd were again on the trail and the Browns' shanty in Tyler was far behind them. Birl whimpered a little at first but he was assured that the wagon had turned around in the night and was now headed in the direction of home. When bedtime of the second night arrived, the procedure of the previous one was repeated. When he next awoke, the boy seemed to sense that something was wrong but that further rebellion was useless. All through the day he sat without a murmur as they slowly traveled on, listening docilely while Boze told him stories or described the pony he would ride when he grew up to be a cowboy like the other men in the outfit. Each hour took him farther from Tyler and nearer the Panhandle toward which they were headed.

When the Pease River was reached, it was swollen far beyond its usual level. Much time was consumed forcing the herd into the water and preparing the wagon for crossing. Birl was removed from his seat beside Boze and put to ride alone on a gentle "paint" the boys had saddled especially for his safe conveyance. After the bridle reins were made fast to the saddle, he was lifted up and tied tightly into his seat; two cowboys then took their places, one on either side of him, to hold with as little slack as possible the rope extending from his saddle horn to theirs,

in an effort to prevent his mount from turning over and submerging its rider midstream.

With final instructions to the little boy to cling to the pony's mane with all his might no matter what happened, the boss plunged into the water to lead the way for the others. Great cottonwood trunks bore down upon them as the horses swam and struggled against an undercurrent that pulled them a mile down the river before they managed to make it across. But, miraculously, men and animals escaped injury and after a while were safely climbing the banks of the opposite side.

This rough baptism by immersion seemed to wash away all Birl's longing for the home he had been forced to leave, and from that day on, with the optimistic adjustment of youth, he ceased to pine for things behind and, as if of his own volition, embarked cheerfully on his career as a cowboy.

The next few days were spent in the sandhill country where only necessary stops were made before reaching the JA pasture on the west side of the drift fence that ran from north to south. There the outfit camped while the boss rode into Clarendon to negotiate a sale. It was not long before he returned with the news that the journey was over. "We'll not be going any further," he said. "I have sold out."

Before dawn of the next morning, the last two days of their long drive were started. On reaching their destination, the cattle were counted and turned loose, and the outfit, after a short rest, rode away with not one word of farewell or explanation to the boy they had stolen but had treated so kindly as they came up the trail from the south.

It has been reported often that Bill Koogle, into whose hands Birl came to remain, paid the price of a cow for him, but the truth of that assertion is not certain. All that is known is that when the others left, Birl stayed behind with the cattle, to find, like them, a new home on the range of the Half Circle K.

The cook at headquarters was a man named Boney, who, in complete disregard of racial prejudice, took the boy to his heart and tried in every way to make up to him for the great wrong done him by his abductors. To his ward went the biggest slice of his hot peach pie and lumps from the contents of the brown sugar barrel, chipped off for substitute candy. The boy was allowed to help with the milking, which he loved, and to work by Boney's side in the garden, where some of the finest melons in the Panhandle grew. Somewhere the cook found an old reader, and it was his pleasure, after the day's work was done, to sit with Birl at his side and, by the dim glow of a smudge light, to teach him to read, write, and spell.

It was also Boney's job to ride the north line because of two water holes that stayed boggy during the rainy season and to go twice a month into town for the mail. As these trips were Birl's chief delight, he was always taken along. One day in the winter, after he had been back and forth to Clarendon many times, he begged to be allowed to make the ride alone, assuring Boney that by that time he was familiar with the way. As it was already cold, his request was refused at first, but, when the cook realized how anxious the little fellow was to prove himself a man, a hesitant consent was given, and Birl was made ready to start. There were only three gates to pass through—two into the horse pasture not far from headquarters and one on the east side through which the road went out of the ranch into the town five miles farther on. Birl's final instructions, after he had been placed astride his gentle pony, were to ride to the gates, open them from his saddle, and ride on without closing them as he was too small to climb back on his horse without assistance.

He had been gone not more than half an hour when the norther that preceded one of the severest storms of the 1880's struck. Luckily, Birl's horse trotted up to the post

office as the snow began to fall. Had he been many minutes later, the boy's fate would have been that of the mail carrier whose driverless horses pulled into town late that afternoon with an empty stage as mute evidence of the tragedy.

Ralph Jefferson, the postmaster, rushed out to carry the boy inside, as he was already too stiff to dismount. He was wrapped in his saddle blanket and placed before the fire, then once again given a drink of the liquid to which he was almost becoming accustomed. He was kept by his white friends until the storm was over and the warm sun made it safe for him to set out for home alone.

In the spring, his friend Boney went to punching cattle, and his place as cook was taken by a man named Clark. When the time to gather beef and to ship came around, hands were short, so the young Birl was given his first real job. As wrangler, it was his business to watch the remuda and occasionally to stand guard at night.

At the end of the summer, Koogle took Birl home to give assistance to his wife. It was the duty of the boy to milk the cow, to wash the dishes, and to act as nurse to children not many years younger than himself. He remained there through that winter and the following one. By that time he was old enough to join the outfit as a permanent hand.

CHAPTER 12

The Law of the West

(In Its Own Peculiar Way)

By a curious omission in the framing of the Republic's constitution, no provision was made for future subdivisions in government. Consequently, Texas remained in its original parts—those established by the Mexicans as municipalities—until after annexation, when thirty-two additional counties were formed.

By an act of the Thirteenth Legislature, the portion of the Panhandle that includes the present counties of Wheeler, Donley, Gray, and Collingsworth was established under the name of Wedgeforth County, but in 1876 this measure was repealed and the existing subdivisions were made. Three years later Wheeler County was organized.

Shortly afterward, because of trouble with cattle rustlers, plans were begun for the formation of the Panhandle Stock Association. At the second meeting, Good-night suggested to those other members who also occupied the range beneath the cap rock that it might be of advantage to all to withdraw from the judiciary control of Wheeler to a point more centrally located. As a result, Donley County was organized, and Clarendon became the county seat.

On April 11, Judge Emmanuel Dobbs, the former buffalo hunter of Mobeetie, swore in the first officers: G. A. Brown, judge; B. H. White, treasurer; Jim Otey, tax assessor; J. H. Parks, surveyor; and Charles Goodnight, Leigh Dyer, and S. B. Nall, commissioners. In 1884, the first election was held in the new county seat, and the following were placed in office: Judge White, county judge; Professor Combs, clerk; Jim Otey, tax assessor; Morris Rosenfield, treasurer; and Al Gentry, sheriff. Unlike most politicians of today, these men earnestly desired to serve the community rather than to be served by it and were especially qualified to fill the places selected for them by their friends.

No more perfect expression of the progressive elements that combined to produce the traditions of the West could be found than in the persons of the four men who contributed in bringing law and order to a disorganized frontier. Henry Fleming of Mobeetie, the Panhandle's first sheriff, was a professional saloonkeeper and gambler but a man of strength and purpose whose word was as good as his marksmanship.

He was followed by "Cap" Arrington, the Panhandle's first ranger captain, wielder of the mailed fist of military law, soldier of fortune, Confederate guerrilla, and cowboy adventurer.

Over Tascosa and its Hog Town Jim East held sway; his code was the code of the West at its wildest. To him sudden death and ribald laughter were both a part of the day's routine. He was able to deal a poker hand with steady nerves while a man lay dead in a corner of the same room. He finished his job no matter the cost but was as kind of heart as he was brave.

In Clarendon there was Al Gentry, gentleman, scion of a distinguished line. His formative years were a blending of the life of diplomatic Washington and the simpler pleasures of the gentle countryside of his native Tennessee. It was in Tennessee that he developed into manhood, nurtured upon the influences of a great house, stimulating guests, numerous slaves, rare works of art, books, music, and of a mother and father who, as lords of all they surveyed, ruled their little domain after the customary manner of the Old South. Al had been taught by a private tutor until he was old enough to be placed in boarding school. While he was there, war broke out, and the boy,

only sixteen at the time, ran away to join the Confederate army. At the close of hostilities he entered Washington University, where he remained until he graduated four years later. Such were his qualifications as a gentleman.

As sheriff, he was true to his convictions and duties, sympathetic, understanding, forceful, and so fearless that his friends boasted even Wild Bill Hickok obeyed when he spoke. In the wanderings that eventually placed Gentry in Texas, he stopped for the night in Abilene, Kansas. Hickok was then the Abilene town marshal and a man of so much action that he was not averse to creating a little excitement himself when things grew too quiet for his taste. Gentry was sitting alone at a table as Hickok and his followers entered the barroom. Seeing before him a newcomer who was not only young but, so the toughs (erroneously) thought, a timid tenderfoot, the leader drew his gun and in a commanding tone suggested that the boy arise and dance to the accompaniment of the bullets directed in a circle around his feet.

Very quietly Gentry got up, standing without flinching until the barrage of fire had ceased. Needless to say, such conduct excited the admiration of Hickok. Considering the joke at an end, he approached the table, put his arm around the young man's shoulder, and drew him toward the bar for a friendly drink. But as they walked

away together, Gentry suddenly stopped, drew his gun, pointed it straight at his adversary, and said very meaningfully, "Now it's my turn. You dance, and dance damn quick, because if you don't, I'll not pepper your feet. I'll shoot you dead!" And, for once, the Kansas marshal danced to the tune of another's playing.

It must not be forgotten that the Panhandle was still sparsely settled and far removed from the general interests of Texas and its governing body at Austin. Laws engendered by the needs of better-known constituents and districts closer in were often harmful to Northwest Texas in their results. The land, in many cases, was taken up in large blocks by cattlemen whose employees were fighters as well as cowhands and whose numbers ran into the hundreds. Each outfit, fortified by its own organized personnel, became a law unto itself, capable of protecting its collective and its individual interests without any assistance whatsoever from the outside.

As the settlers, men of less property and power, increased in number, a more established procedure was required to preserve their rights. It was then that the first counties were organized and a legal routine was resorted to. But, in the beginning, the law was so laxly enforced that it commanded respect from neither its administrators nor its beneficiaries.

The judicial body itself was composed of men of the same temperament as the cattle pioneers; otherwise they would not have chosen the rough frontier as the place to practice their profession. Being of the same temperament, they had an understanding of the people and the land and were actuated primarily by motives that did not always coincide with the letter of the law as written by less sympathetic politicians at the capital. They lived and functioned generally according to the dictates of their primitive society rather than the conventional demands of their profession. Consider the judge and sheriff who, during a long cross-country trip, found themselves lost and without food.

"What shall we do?" asked the latter.

"Kill a beef," replied the judge.

"We can't do that," demurred the other. "That's stealing. They'll get us for it."

To which the judge responded, "I'd like to know who in the hell can get us. I'm the judge, and you are the sheriff. We are the law."

Those were the days before rigid bar examinations, and the qualities necessary to make a jurist were more often common sense and personality than erudition and specific training. Anyone who desired could apply for a license. After a superficial hearing, conducted in the presence of the court, or not, as stipulated by a committee composed of three other men who often had entered the profession with as little preparation as the applicant, the license was usually awarded.

In the entire district there were not more than seventy-five persons available for jury duty, and among this number the majority were not qualified legally, as they were neither freeholders nor landowners and, in many cases, had no desire to be either. Because so many of the inhabitants were connected by birth, marriage, or denominational interests or were drifting cowboys in the employ of large operators, any case that came to trial was likely to be a family affair, with the judge and jury so closely related in some way to the plaintiff or to the defendant as to make an unbiased decision impossible. From these conditions there arose a disregard for the law and a levity toward its administration that made the term of court not a serious time for the adjustment of the difficulties of the people but a festive occasion like a county fair.

The sessions themselves were entirely informal. There were frequent recesses in which everyone concerned, the accused included, moved upstairs to partake of a hot toddy mixed in a large pitcher kept for the purpose. And, when the trial had ended, if the condemned man on his way to the penitentiary, on passing a saloon, happened to hint at a last drink to the law-enforcers to whom he was handcuffed, the response usually was, "You do make the most seasonable suggestions."

The decision of the court was often reached in a manner equally unusual and was the result chiefly of the inclinations of the presiding judge, who arbitrarily assumed the prerogative of adjusting matters in a manner best suited to the needs of the day, with little regard for legality.

But, in spite of laxity and lack of dignity, the men in charge of the proceedings were among the Panhandle's most brilliant minds. G. A. Brown, or "Gyp" as he was nicknamed, held his appointment as Donley's first judge only long enough to preside once, before moving to Austin to advance the interests of the cattle country and its voters. While there, he was appointed to the supreme bench but he died before assuming office.

Many other famous men traveled by buggy or stage between Mobeetie, Tascosa, and Clarendon during the 1880's: among them Grigsby, Plemmons, Patton, Wallace, Dills, Wiley, and Frank Willis, who received from Governor Roberts the appointment as Wheeler County's first judge, an office he held with honor until 1891. Willis was born in Indiana, moved from there to Missouri, then to Kansas, and finally to Texas to become Northwest Texas' first judicial head.

Of all the lawyers, the most colorful were J. N. Browning, W. H. Woodman, and Temple Houston. Although entirely unlike in personality, they possessed one attribute in common—an ability to sway an audience at will. Houston was one of the younger children of Sam Houston; he was born in the Governor's Mansion during the "Raven's" administration as governor. He was handsome, brilliant, and charming, and, with the additional heritage of his father's prestige, could have possessed any honor that Texas had to bestow had he chosen to use his talents to that end. He was very tall, with blue eyes and sandy hair that he wore in curls hanging on his shoulders. He walked with short, nervous steps and allowed his head to drop slightly forward on his chest, giving him the romantic appearance of preoccupation. His dress was a mixture of Western informality and legal dignity, consisting of cowboy boots, a Prince Albert coat, and a white Stetson, which he changed on rare occasions to black. He spoke in a voice attuned to play on the heart strings of any audience, and, when he arose to plead his case, the opposing lawyer knew that no power in the West could alter the verdict imposed on the jury by his appealing oratory.

Judge J. N. Browning, or "Honest Jim," was the Panhandle's rabid reformer. His Sundays were spent in teaching the Scripture to girls of the Methodist church, his weekdays in fighting, in every possible way, gambling and other frontier vices, although some claimed he was the best poker player in the county. His evangelical efforts were greatly resented by the rougher element at Mobeetie, but even threats of death did not deter him or lessen his zeal. He had grown up on a farm in Kansas and moved to Fort Griffin at the time when it was wildest. There he developed from a cowboy into a prosperous cattleman and from choice took up the study of law. He was a very large man and a popular orator whose powerful voice played a conspicuous part in the later politics of Northwest Texas.

Judge Woodman came from Henrietta and boasted that he had never owned a law book. But, whatever his source of ability—the printed page, experience, personality, or intuition—he possessed it to such a degree that, like Houston, he rarely lost a case. He was a man of striking appearance, with an expressive face, keen blue eyes, and jet black hair worn in a long, straight bob. At some time or other, he had taken vocal lessons and not only sang but also spoke like a professional and acted equally well. He was the Panhandle's wittiest and most ingenious lawyer and had at his command whatever was required to win.

"If tears were necessary, he could weep volumes, and, if Biblical verses were advantageous," so his associates said, "he could quote Scripture until the sun went down."

The first grand jury was convened in 1884. There were so few real felonies that this dignified body was forced to indict for misdemeanors, some of which were not only amusing of themselves but doubly so because of the persons involved. The first dockets were filled with the names of the town's most prominent citizens: the doctor for practicing without a license, a minister for perjury, one judge for indecent exposure, another for "taking and using estray mules," and all the cowboys for gambling.

As was to be expected in a cattle country, many of the cases were for unlawful fencing or grazing but, strange as it may seem, rarely for theft. Although theoretically the cattle thief was considered lower than the murderer, cattle stealing by individuals was a common practice. However, when a man grew too bold or too careless, the other "righteous" citizens sometimes formed what they called a "necktie party," and a hanging resulted unless the culprit was very quick-witted and glib of tongue.

Once a highly respected member of Clarendon society was caught rustling, and, although his apprehenders were his intimate friends, they lost no time in rushing him to a spot out from town where stood a cottonwood tree of suitable height. After dismounting, they proceeded without apology to fasten around his neck a noose conveniently fashioned from one of their lariats. But, at this point, a difficulty they had not foreseen arose. Although all were eager parties to the deed in progress, at the last not one was willing himself to draw the rope. In their hesitation the doomed man glimpsed a chance to escape. Having remembered the Biblical tale of the fallen woman and the accusers who could not cast the first stone, he said slyly, with mock humility, "Why don't you let the one among you who can honestly say he has never committed the same offense hang me?" And his friends, like the men of long ago, dropped their heads in shame and silently rode away.

There were lively times when court was in session, and one town was privileged to play host to most of the Panhandle. Every private home was crowded with guests, and the hotel overflowed into the yard where tents were filled with plaintiffs, witnesses, attorneys, and jurors, all of whom were accompanied by their wives, as the women chose this occasion for shopping and visiting with friends.

Even so, all the business was not of a frivolous nature, particularly as conflicts between cowman and farmer grew more acute. However, the character of the case in no way affected the procedure of the governing body. The law of the West and its administrators continued to rule in "its and their peculiar way," according to the dictates of a "government of the people, for the people, and by the people."

CHAPTER 13

Harbingers of Change

(The Preacher, the Teacher, and the Doctor)

IF the first frame building in the colony ever served the purpose for which it was erected in the beginning, there is little evidence other than an occasional mention of an "institute of learning," known as Allentown Academy. Religious services were not in keeping with the requirements of the frontier even in a settlement where the prevalence of ministers gave rise to the derisive appellation of "Saints' Roost." Children were few and were needed for duties more urgent than the learning of the three "R's."

It has been impossible to gather a connected story of the development of the school. Therefore, the recital of events up to the date of the county's organization must be accepted not as a statement of facts but rather as a credible account based upon a few authentic occurrences.

From the time of W. A. Allen's marriage to Carhart's sister Emma, the lives of the two men followed much the same course, for Allen was also a Methodist preacher and an impractical theorist as well. But, unlike his more forceful relative by marriage, he lacked the initiative to bring to completion any of his many amorphous plans. As a result, he achieved little other than the personal satisfaction of basking in the reflection of Carhart's activities or following in the shadow of his large and pompous wife, who, had she been a character from Dickens, would have been described as a "woman of great presence." Whether Allen's removal from Iowa to Texas was by chance or at his own desire is not known. Anyway, when his brother-in-law was made presiding elder of the Denison district, it was Allen who assumed charge of the pastorate left vacant by the change.

If the reader recalls, this was the year in which the Sherman church was erected and in which the idea of the colony began to take material form. Allen, like other ministers of that period, considered the education of the young to be as much a part of his obligation to the church as the spiritual welfare of their elders. Therefore, when approached, he was an eager party to the idea of establishing a temperance colony and a Methodist college on the plains. Carhart, in ignorance of the country and its characteristics, had never a doubt as to the success of his plan and, as usual, was able through his own enthusiasm to convert those around him to his point of view. Therefore, when he and Allen set off for the West, it was with the full consent and cooperation of the church. The one was to establish the town; the other, having been removed with the bishop's permission "to the Clarendon district as principal of Clarendon Seminary," was to found a school that, under his leadership, would develop into a great seat of learning and help convert the frontier to Methodism.

But the era of education had not yet reached the Panhandle, so after a few months Allen was forced to abandon the idea. In 1881, he "departed town" to resume preaching in connection with a charge in Fort Worth. His ambition to found a school was a worthy one and failed chiefly because it was too far in advance of the times. The glory of achievement was denied him. Therefore he is not remembered as the successful builder of a college, but merely as the man who became the Panhandle's first teacher and gave to Clarendon the distinction of having the first school in the region, if only a school of sorts.

It was not long before the unused schoolhouse was put to practical service, being rented to Major Van Horn for use as the town's first store, after which it is doubtful if education would have received further attention for some time to come had not the preacher's departure coincided with the arrival of the colony's new manager, Judge White, who considered established facilities for the training of the children present a necessary part of any livable community.

A few months later, the Stockmen's Association chose to convene in Clarendon, and Judge White took occasion to call the need for a school to the attention of Goodnight, who in turn presented it to that organization. As there were no state funds yet available for educational purposes in Donley County, it was necessary to raise the money by subscription. As a matter of fact, not one of the cattlemen at that time had a child of school age, but this did not prevent the immediate adoption of a resolution to establish a school fund. T. R. Dickson, the secretary, was instructed to figure the cost per capita and to mail individual bills to each member of the Association.

A teacher was engaged, and soon the first public school in the Panhandle was in full running order. In the picket house built for Ed Carhart and his press, on planks nailed across drygoods boxes, sat the original class of ten pupils, all children of the colonists: the White boys, the Allen girls, the Phillips boys, Wally Parks, and the Wagner children. The following year they were moved to more comfortable quarters in an upstairs room of the courthouse.

In September, 1884, following his election to office in

the spring, Judge White ordered that "Donley County be established as a school district, that the said district be numbered as one and the boundaries be the boundaries of the county."

In March of the following year, the school lands in Hockley were sold to J. W. Nunn, thus establishing the nucleus of a permanent fund. As soon as possible, a frame building was erected under the direction of the school trustee, Morris Rosenfield. Tom Martindale, a cowboy from the Heart Ranch, was elected teacher, a "good bull-whacker gone wrong," as one of his pupils described him. And, at last, education was fixed upon a solid groundwork.

In the year following his election as principal of the nonexistent Clarendon Seminary, Allen was "assigned" to the town by the conference, which explains the report of the missionary Garvis that "Clarington [sic], a point around which has gathered a group of Methodist ministers, supports a pastor brought by the colonists when they migrated," and proves that even though there was no active congregation, the colony had the first church and the first appointed minister. In 1880, he was made a "supernumerary preacher" and, as the reader knows, was absent in 1881 and then in 1882 returned to the colony with Carhart after they had been "located at their own request."

During the twelve months following their withdrawal from the church, the two men were too engrossed with temporal affairs to concern themselves much with religion, so it was as if in answer to direct need that another Methodist preacher happened into the colony during that same year.

Although he had been forced from active duty and had taken residence in the West because of ill health, the Reverend Graham, the Virginian, became from the moment of his arrival Clarendon's minister ex-officio, burying the dead, marrying the young, and preaching in town and out, as he traveled the cowtrails of the Panhandle in performance of his self-imposed duties. He might well have been called the "marrying parson" because it was in his rock dugout that most of the wedding rites were read, often amid circumstances that made ludicrous an otherwise serious occasion.

It was there that Al Gentry and Sella Phillips were married during one of the worst sandstorms known to the Panhandle. Graham had been in town all day and arrived home in the late afternoon to find one end of his simple abode entirely blown away and the part that remained covered with rocks, adobe mortar, and debris. But a quick housecleaning was undertaken, and all was tidy and in readiness when the prospective bride and groom drove in

HB

after sundown, so covered with sand that they bore more resemblance to Mexicans than to their natural selves.

Down on the Red River, near the Shoe Bar Ranch, was a family named Nichols, leading the life of nomads as they pitched their tent, then moved it again whenever their herd found a better grazing ground. Living with them was Nichols's young half-sister, Minerva, who, it was decided, should be subjected to more civilizing influences than those of a trail camp. Having arranged for her to live in the home of the Murdocks, her brother established her in Clarendon under the tutelage of Professor Combs and his wife. One of the first persons she met after arriving in Clarendon was Gene Mosher, who had recently left the Goodnight outfit to become a hand at the Heart horse ranch. Their courtship was fast and furious, and, before the advantages of town had even had time to take effect, the two stopped by the parson's to be married, very casually, all during the course of a horseback ride. As they started off after the ceremony, the bride's cowpony began to pitch, and, for a few minutes, it looked as if her wedding day might end disastrously. But she was an excellent horsewoman; she held her seat and was soon able to lope off down the road. Among Minerva's possessions were ten head of cows and calves which Gene started to gather the next day. Having got them back to Clarendon, he opened the town's first butcher shop, in which he did a thriving business—at least, while the wife's dowry lasted.

But, informal though the general atmosphere was, Graham was meticulous to a superlative degree about matters of the law and the church. The marriage of S. A. Watson and Mrs. Cooper, the divorced sister of Bill Ross, was solemnized at the home of a friend who lived far out of McClellan. As the buggies of the bridal pair and the minister approached town, the parson remembered that, since the license had been issued in Donley County, legal procedure demanded that the wedding take place there, too, and, unluckily, the house from which he had just come lay over the line in Gray County. He immediately pulled his horses to a halt, alighted, and with all seriousness reread the rites—to the amusement of all concerned, except himself.

As for formal services of worship, whenever or however conducted, they were under the auspices of the Northern Methodist denomination. Carhart, when present, presided, looking very dignified and devout with his sideburns and long ministerial coat, even if he was not always quite as convincing a preacher as he might have been. Such was the case one Sunday when, with tear-filled eyes, he rebuked members of the congregation for having desecrated the preceding Lord's Day by fishing, apparently forgetful of the fact that on that same holy Sabbath his cowboys had participated, with his full consent, in a large roundup and branding.

Directly in front of the minister's house hung the five-hundred–pound bell that rang the worshippers to service. Carhart had first seen it on exhibit in Cincinnati where he was attending a church conference and, after much difficulty, had purchased it for two hundred and fifty dollars. It was his passion from the first, and nothing gave him more pleasure than to listen to its great metallic voice as it pealed forth across the prairies. Any Sunday little Willie Murdock could be seen swinging from the bell rope as he sounded the call to God in a heathen land.

With the assistance of Mrs. White and her portable organ, Sunday school was held regularly. Finally, in 1885, the bishop assigned a second minister to the district. Great must have been his astonishment to find on reaching his new pastorate that the only house of worship in an obstinately temperate town was a saloon. Sometime after the establishment of the "Christian colony," the *Tascosa Pioneer* ran an editorial asserting that "prohibition will not succeed in any state, county, precinct, or town where there is any life, any liability of business, or anything approaching the semblance of a boom."[1] Although all property in

[1] *Tascosa Pioneer*, March 30, 1887.

Clarendon was first sold with a stipulation forbidding liquor on the premises at any time, it was inevitable that sooner or later an attempt would be made to establish a saloon in a community that agreed generally in attitude with the *Pioneer*.

In the early 1880's, there happened to be living in Mobeetie a carpenter by the name of Andy Jackson, who, during the slack months of winter when he was unable to follow his trade, worked up and down the creeks chopping and storing ice for future hot weather use. As one of his main dugouts was on Carroll Creek, he and his young partner, William Fleming, often passed through Clarendon, not to tarry, however, as no public place of amusement was to be found there.

With the approach of spring, the idea suggested itself to the two men, who had personally suffered from the lack, that the ice already gathered might be put to better advantage by starting a refreshment parlor in the colony. They went immediately to work. By June, a frame building, twenty-five by fifty feet, had been completed and made ready for use as a pool hall and soft drink stand. But hard liquor alone could quench the prairie thirst, and business was none too good. One day, by chance, the discouraged proprietors learned that the prohibition ruling could not be enforced. With the greatest of haste, they began the changes necessary to convert their place into the county's first saloon.

However, the original intention of the colony's founder was not to be so easily thwarted. When Donley County was organized shortly afterward, "local option" was put into effect, and Carhart immediately persuaded the more loyal of his supporters to vote liquor out. Then, in true fidelity to purpose, as if in apology to God, he transformed the saloon into the home of Clarendon's first established church. Thus it happened that the new minister delivered his opening address on a pulpit which, after all, was only a bar hidden from view by a large wagon sheet.

The Rev. J. J. Cooper, for such was the name of the Englishman who became the pastor, arrived shortly before Christmas. As his wife and baby son did not join him until spring, he kept bachelor quarters in a one-room "adobe" near the Parks's house. He was a good talker and very popular with the congregation, but the customary two-year period ended about the time of the town's removal, and he was transferred to Mobeetie, leaving George Richardson in charge in the new Clarendon. Among the inhabitants there were several staunch Episcopal adherents who, with the assistance of Bishop Garrett, made a noble attempt to change the accepted faith of the colony. But, in spite of their efforts, the colony remained what Carhart intended it to be—a Methodist town.

During most of the colony's existence there was no resident physician, but the life of the community moved on very comfortably nonetheless, for the pioneer, in sickness as in everything else, was a self-sufficient individual. The girls learned early the gentle art of nursing: how to dose babies with coal oil and paregoric and to rub congested chests with a mixture of tallow, camphor, and turpentine. Every woman was a midwife and boasted nerves that never flinched in the presence of blood or anguish. The men were adept at "first aid," and they ministered to the usual needs as well as any more skilled professional.

But of more importance than their training was their attitude toward life in general and themselves in particular. They possessed a stoicism that enabled them to take hardship as a matter of course and to accept discomfort and pain in the same manner. Death was not a much-dreaded end but an inevitable event that one approached without fear and experienced with dignity. With fatalistic philosophy, they believed a certain thing happened or did not happen, and there was not much to be done about it either way. In an atmosphere of that sort, the innately weak soon learned to simulate strength, having discovered from experience that the person with great self-control had neither an understanding of nor a sympathy for the possessor of a temperament less phlegmatic or of sensibilities more highly attuned than his own.

When the need for a doctor became evident, it was again Goodnight's wealth and influence that contributed to the colony's development by making it possible for one to come, as his assistance had made possible the establishment of a public school. Whether such benevolent actions were the result of interest in the region's progress or of the affection the man in question bore his wife is a matter entirely beside the point.

The early years of Mrs. Goodnight's life in the Panhandle were occupied wholly in caring for the physical and spiritual welfare of her large family of "boys." Accompanied by the small black bag that served as her medical kit, "Aunt Molly" made regular daily rounds, stopping wherever necessary to cheer the discouraged or lonely, or to minister to the sick with the practical remedies learned during her long residence on the frontier. However, as she grew older and the number of ranch hands multiplied many times over, she began to feel the need of skilled assistance. At her suggestion, her husband, who had great respect for her judgment and was always agreeable to any project in which she was interested, approached the citizens of Clarendon concerning the ways and means of procuring a doctor for their particular part of the country.

As the nearest physician was located at Mobeetie, some fifty miles distant, the idea met the hearty approval of everyone, and a committee was formed to take immediate action. Realizing that their greatest difficulty lay in persuading a competent man to relinquish his practice for the uncertain returns of a sparsely populated area whose patients were few and far between, they set about raising through subscription a fund to be offered in addition to any income derived through professional efforts. With Goodnight's contribution forming a substantial nucleus, the goal of a thousand dollars was soon reached.

The first doctor the committee approached was a practitioner in East Texas, one whom Carhart had known during the time of his Dallas pastorate. Many unsuccessful attempts had already been made to persuade this man to join the colony, but the minister, undaunted, was eager to try again, especially as he knew him to be not only an excellent physician and a man of high integrity but also—and this in Carhart's opinion was the qualification of most importance—a devout Methodist.

Jerome Daniel Stocking was born December 24, 1849, in the little town of Lisbon in upstate New York.

Having graduated from Potsdam Normal School, he enrolled at the University of Michigan to undertake the study of medicine. Soon after receiving his degree, he was forced through ill health to forsake the East. He made the long move to Texas, where he taught school in Waco before settling in Lawrence to take up the practice of his profession. Meanwhile, he married, and his wife developed tuberculosis. Consequently, on hearing again from Carhart, he did not, as before, discourage the overtures, but wrote in reply that he would take the matter under serious consideration, as he felt the change to a higher altitude might be of benefit to Mrs. Stocking, whose strength was failing fast.

Shortly afterward, Carhart, having heard that Morris Rosenfield was leaving soon to buy goods in Chicago, arranged with him to stop over in Dallas for a conference with the doctor in the hope that a personal interview might accomplish more than previous negotiations by mail. On stepping from the train in the Dallas station one day in 1885, the merchant recognized with ease the dignified, scholarly looking gentleman as the man he had come to see and introduced himself by saying, "I am Morris Rosenfield of Clarendon who has come as a committee of one to discuss the proposition made to you by Mr. Carhart."

Stocking explained at once that his chief concern was for the comfort of his family, naively adding that his wife was a "refined lady," and he wondered if there would be accorded her out West the kind of treatment to which she had been accustomed in the more civilized region of Lawrence. Rosenfield hastened to assure him that at no time would she or their boys be subjected to the slightest indignities among a people who were gentle of heart in spite of their rough exterior. As additional inducement, the merchant explained fully the $1,000 bonus arranged by the committee, thus eliminating the doctor's two major objections. By the end of the interview Stocking had promised to go immediately to Clarendon, where he would complete the final negotiations provided he was still favorably inclined after having seen the town. True to his word, he arrived in Clarendon in a week or so, having driven alone in his buggy over the entire distance of several hundred miles; the deal was closed.

Very soon the doctor, his wife, and their two young sons, Fred and Roy, were established in a house bought from the Phillips family, and there they lived most happily until the death of the "refined lady" the following year. Mrs. Stocking's sister, Alice Hubbell, cared for the widower's house and the sons until her marriage to Joe Huffman, after which the little boys were placed in the Mur-

dock home and Dr. Stocking turned for solace to the work of lessening the pain and grief of the many people who, during his short residence in their midst, had already learned to rely upon him for spiritual as well as physical assistance. His buggy was a familiar sight anywhere within a hundred and fifty miles of town. Countless discomforts were soothed by the pills he mixed in a mortar bowl in his "drugstore" in the Carhart house where, until his coming, the patent medicines of J. W. Carhart had been offered as the chief remedies for the country's ills.

Death did not visit the frontier more often than elsewhere, but when it did appear there were few of the formalities of civilization to soften the grim features of its tragic face. When the Koogle baby died, Sella Gentry and Vashta Parks lined the miniature hand-hewn box with a white cashmere shawl, carefully preserved by a neighbor as a memento of happier days. Carrie Koogle was a Catholic, and her childlike terror at ushering a loved one into eternity without the ministrations of a priest was pathetic.

One spring, when the McKinney baby was two or three, the Heart outfit set out to drive a herd to market. After the cattle had been on the road several days, the foreman Al McKinney and his wife and child decided to follow in a buggy in order that some additional instructions might be given the wagon boss. Fayette McKinney was a playful youngster and a general favorite with the boys. As they sat around the campfire the first night after overtaking the outfit, someone called his name, and he started across the prairie to seek the friend he could hear but could not see. He had run only a few steps when an indistinct noise, like the rattling of shells in the wind, broke the stillness of the night. There was no mistaking that ominous sound. The woman shrieked, and Al jumped for his boy, but it was too late. The rattlesnake had struck —and Fayette died in his mother's arms as they raced back to town across the prairie.

Dr. Stocking's first case was an epileptic, a young girl at the JA headquarters, married, and the mother of a child, though only fifteen. During an attack she had fainted and fallen into an open fire. Before her rescuers could drag her off the live coals, she had been fatally burned. One of the cowboys had hurried into town, but, by the time he was able to ride the distance horseback and drive back with the doctor, she was almost dead. During her last agonies, she spoke only once, apologizing for the screams which in her pain she had been unable to suppress.

Dental work also fell to the new doctor's lot, as the only dentists were bungling itinerants whose outstanding claims to distinction were the exorbitant fees collected during their occasional visits to town. Previous to the doctor's arrival, the local butcher had sometimes been forced to turn professional. When such an occasion arose, he would, without apology, lay down upon his bloody meat block the huge knife of his trade, pick up the rusty forceps he kept on hand for the purpose, and, by some means or other, manage to extract the molar from the throbbing jaw of the agonized but grateful customer.

The doctor, who was almost as unskilled as the butcher in the dental line, was asked one day by a frightened patient if the extraction would be painful, to which he jokingly replied, "If it does *not* hurt, I'll not *charge* you a cent." The woman concerned happened to be both economical and literal, so, after giving the matter due consideration, she settled herself with determination in the chair before him, and there she sat without movement or change of expression until he had finished and both the tooth and his instrument lay on the table at his side. She then arose, straightened her clothes, thanked him, and walked out. The matter of a fee was never mentioned by either.

After the coming of the new town and its restricted district, many trips were made to the sandhills to sew up wounds received in drunken frays or to prevent the death of some remorseful girl who had attempted to end a life tragically begun. But all was not sorrowful. There were amusing incidents, sometimes even in the presence of death, as when the old Dutchman looked into the face of his deceased wife and said, "Doc, I believe it would have been easier for me to give up my best span of mules than that old woman."

There were also occasional days of leisure when grief and suffering were put aside for the simple pleasures of life. Most of all, the doctor liked to enjoy the companionship of a few congenial friends or to wander up and down the banks of the creek in search of fish with his two adoring "little socks" following close upon his heels.

CHAPTER 14

Panhandle Society

(At the Court of the Free Grass Empire)

WITH the passage of years many new families came to reside in Donley, and the colony underwent the gradual change that comes to all places and people as they encounter those great milestones of life—birth, marriage, financial success and failure, and death. The years had been happy ones, in which all were bound together in a friendly intimacy possible only in primitive and isolated communities. The major wealth of the region, as was to be expected, was soon concentrated among a few, but it altered very slightly the status of those who did or did not possess it. Everyone prospered to a mild degree; dire poverty was unknown, and social lines were too indistinctly drawn to be of much consequence. However, with the commencement of a new period and the coming of women like Mrs. Benjamin White, trained to give proper respect to the amenities of life, the character of the country began to alter perceptibly.

On the evening of December 23, 1881, soon after the completion of the White House, Ed Carhart and Mary Estella Brewer became Donley County's first bride and groom. In the absence of the bride's parents, who had moved to Mobeetie, the judge and his wife acted as host and hostess for the reception that followed the ceremony. From beginning to end, the affair was conducted with a formality previously unheard of in those parts and prophetic of the order to come.

Reverend Carhart read the service in the lobby of the new hotel, which was filled to capacity with guests. The bride wore a frock of tan and blue checkered silk, with many ruffles and large puffed sleeves. Her veil, as a real one was not available, was a lace scarf lent for the occasion by Carhart's wife, who was in town on one of her rare visits. The young couple left the following day for Mobeetie. There, as the chief event of their honeymoon, they visited the picture gallery at the fort in order that the bride might be photographed in her wedding finery and the jewelry of brass which the photographer kept on hand for special subjects like her.

By 1885, eight or ten daughters of resident families had reached the mature ages of fifteen or sixteen and around them centered the social life of the town and the attentions of the district's fifty or more eligible bachelors.

Among these were Mrs. Goodnight's brothers, the Dyer boys; Charlie Wright; and Jesse Wynne, who had come from Terrell to work on the Barton horse ranch but later joined the Heart outfit. Ben Chamberlain, a nephew of Judge White, was a general favorite because he danced well and had a habit of keeping his pockets filled with sweetmeats from Rosenfield's store where he clerked. Among the Britishers were Irish Dick Walsh, who became manager of the JA under Mrs. Adair's ownership, and Charlie O'Donel, sent west by his uncle, Count Kearney, as undercover agent to protect the foreign interests of the Clarendon Land Investment and Agency Company.

After Judge and Mrs. White moved from the hotel, much of the entertaining took place in their new house. Their friends dropped in often of an evening to play, sing, or recite. Besides these informal gatherings, there were oyster suppers, horseback rides, and spelling bees. At this last, everyone, big and little, stood up together to compete, and, as the words came faster and faster and one participant after another dropped out, the fun grew hilarious.

As a matter of course, the oysters at the suppers were canned, but this made little difference to the healthy appetite of the plains. Sometimes these affairs were not purely social but were sponsored by the women of the church to raise money for some worthy cause, at which times they took on more than usual dignity with an opening talk by the minister, the singing of hymns, and an occasional solo. Sometimes an auction was held and a tidy sum raised if the article in question was a rarity, like the first box of strawberries brought in from the Murdock farm as an exhibition of the agricultural possibilities of the Panhandle.

Once even a Shakespeare Club was organized to meet every two weeks for the discussion of the plays of the "bard," but blank verse was not a characteristic expression of the locality, and the club met a quick death.

Besides dancing, amateur theatricals were the most popular form of amusement. The people never tired of taking part or looking on, and, when the performances were too infrequent, the editor of the newspaper would inquire, "When will the Dramatic Society give its next entertainment?" It is interesting to note what a generation whose progeny bred such men as Pinter and Ionesco chose as its favorite plays; their significance is best described by some of the titles: *Down on the Rio Grande, Union Depot,* and *Old Maids' Convention.*

When a suitable drama was not found, tableaux were resorted to. These required much more ingenuity in production, as in *Bluebeard's Wives,* which required tying the hair of the victims to the ceiling, chalking their faces to the pallor of death, and hiding their bodies behind a sheet. Pharaoh's daughter, in *Moses in the Bulrushes*, sat draped in a paisley shawl looking into a basket and surrounded by real reeds gathered from the banks of a muddy hole on the creek. A sunset glow, achieved by means of a lantern with a colored shade, softened the scene, and all would have been perfect had not the infant Moses, who was borrowed for the act, performed in a manner most unbecoming to one destined to lead God's chosen people out of the wilderness into the Promised Land. On another occasion a young married woman played a risen angel in *Easter Dawn* and, through some inspired contraption, appeared suspended in mid-air with no apparent means of support other than large, silk-covered cardboard wings. She repeated the success of this role later in the evening when she hovered over the *Rock of Ages*, to which two of her friends clung with considerable awkwardness and uncertainty.

Sometimes it was not a member of the cast but someone in the audience who made the hit of the performance, as when Temple Houston entered with Mrs. Allen on his arm. She was gowned in extreme décolletage, and he wore his customary Prince Albert, boots, and Stetson, to which he had added, for formality, a pair of white kid gloves and a necktie of rattlesnake skin. When they made their appearance in the doorway, the cowboys arose as a man to stamp and whistle and throw their hats into the air. But the demonstration did not perturb Houston in the slightest. With much nonchalance he continued down the aisle to his seat in the same manner that Lord Chesterfield might have employed in placing his "lady" in her seat at Covent Garden.

As there was so few of them, the children were allowed to participate in the pleasure of their elders who, in turn, joined in the children's games. Judge White and Al Gentry were as good at marbles as the best of them but got very angry when they found a youngster cheating. Tod Lewis, the latest to arrive from the East, knew the rules of the more formal games and was often called in to settle an argument as to "how it was done in Washington," or to define the special business of each fellow who made up the "baseball nine." "Bantie," a favorite sport, took much courage when the leader was a daredevil who attempted anything from high jumps to rolling down the longest hill nailed tight inside a barrel.

As each boy approached manhood, his one idea was to be a cowboy. Any old "plug" that could be caught was used for a mount while a pet pup served as "calf" for the amateur roper. When, however, the aspirant considered himself proficient enough to engage the assistance of a frisky calf, he was likely, before all was over, to find himself in a daze on the ground, tangled in the wrong end of a rope being manipulated not by himself but by the animal he had so successfully caught a few minutes before.

For less exciting amusement there were wild plums and grapes to be gathered in the summer and long and frequent swims in the creek behind the judge's house. To break the monotony, the Salt Fork rose on periodic rampages, and, when least expected, Indians passed through on their way to beg buffalo from Goodnight. Sometimes, as a great favor, the little Stockings, Haven Graham, or Maxie Rosenfield were allowed to carry the guns for the big boys when they hunted in the hills. There were roundups and picnics, and, when these were ended, it was time to look forward to the coming of Christmas.

About the middle of each December, it was usual for the newspaper to state that "A meeting largely attended was held on Saturday night at eight o'clock. Mr. —— was made the chairman, and committees were selected to conduct the work of preparation. Immediately upon adjournment, soliciting was industriously commenced, and, in a few minutes, one lady had collected twelve or fifteen dollars." Later in the week a large cedar was cut from the nearest canyon and hauled in to hold the many presents. Everyone was invited, and no one was forgotten, although the girls always received the greatest number of gifts. One year, when Mr. Hecox was playing Santa Claus, he unexpectedly came across a package bearing his own name, and, realizing that the children's fun would be spoiled if his identity were disclosed, he announced solemnly that this gift was for someone who was not able to be present, as he had been forced to haul a load of wood; at this one youngster in the audience said to his mother in a voice audible to all, "I don't want to grow up if they make you work on Christmas tree night."

The Fourth of July was the occasion for the biggest picnic of the year, and the roundups were the gayest of the summer affairs. The ranch host on whose pasture the work was in progress supplied the barbecued beef, which, together with the homemade pies, cakes, and jellies brought by the women, made up the feast. Buggies and wagons started from town or neighboring ranches in the early morning hours to assure each family a timely arrival. The men liked to take an active part in all the work of roping, cutting, and branding, while their wives gossiped, admired the newest baby, and exchanged with friends the newspapers and magazines collected since their last meeting. After the noonday meal, there were songs and recitations and stunts performed by the exhibitionists for the amusement of those less confident. If the work was finished early enough in the afternoon, a horse race was staged by the cowboys as an exciting climax.

Races were also frequently held in town on the flat behind the cemetery, and, although gambling with dice or cards was an offense to be investigated by the grand jury, betting on horses was judged perfectly acceptable. In those days, the rules were squarely made and squarely followed, and animal flesh and horsemanship alone decided the winner. At Christmas the town offered a substantial money reward, and excitement ran high. Wagons and buggies, filled with sedate married folk, stood in rows on the sidelines; boisterous cowboys crowded behind to cheer their favorite as the riders raced across the prairie to a given point straight ahead; and the girls added an incongruous note to the picture, seated gracefully on sidesaddles in skirts so long they almost touched the ground and wearing "braize" veils that floated in streamers held aloft by the wind.

When the herds were very large, the roundups lasted several days and were followed at night by a big dance on an out-of-door platform built especially for the occasion. The cowboys furnished the music themselves with their fiddles, guitars, and jew's-harps. Square dances were the order of the day, with the schottische, the polka, and lively Virginia reels for a climax. Bill Ross and his two sisters, both divorcees, were always present. As the girls were as stout as he was huge, they literally "shook the floor" with their enthusiasm when two of them danced together.

Although there was much drinking among the men, it was never done at times like these but rather when they were out with members of their own sex. There has never existed a class more respectful, as a whole, of womanhood than the boys of the old West. There was no halfway ground with them; a woman was either good or she was bad, and a gentleman acted accordingly.

In town the old saloon served for the ballroom as well as for the church. If a report of the coming affair was circulated in time, the boys came on horseback, possibly as far as a hundred miles, to dance most of the night, and then in the early morning to start their long ride back without one moment's sleep. The girls made great preparations. Dresses were hastily devised of muslin adorned with ribbon bows of the same color as the wildflower selected for the hair.

Cosmetics were unknown, but the ingenious female could paint her lips with the juice of a berry or petal, blacken her eyebrows with a burnt match, and whiten her skin by an application of cornstarch or flour. Her hair, however, was a more difficult problem as a hue not desired by the owner was a matter to be grieved over but never changed. The wife of one of the town's leading judges was looked at slightly askance because it was whispered that her beautiful bronze locks were artificially tinted by the use of soda shampoos and the sun's hot rays—an almost immoral procedure in the eyes of the other women.

Sometimes oyster suppers preceded the dancing, but more often the repast was served at midnight and consisted of such delicacies as smothered quail, wild turkey with dressing, antelope steaks, red beans, dried-apple pies, and an ample supply of homemade wild-grape wine. Parson Allen and Mrs. Allen and Judge White and Mrs. White did not dance but always went to look on, and young couples like the Lords and the Olivers drove in from their ranches. Such were the wholesome, simple pleasures of a pioneer people.

In the fall of 1886, Bruce McClelland and his bride reached Clarendon and stopped to rest overnight before going on to the new house he had built in her honor out on the Kelley Creek. She was the daughter of an Alabama physician, a beautiful girl with soft brown eyes, dark curls, and skin like the petals of the magnolia blossoms that grew so profusely in her native state. Without conscious effort, Lottie White had paved the way well for the

— HDBugbee —

the coming of this other gentlewoman who in a few, short months was to be the social arbiter and leader of fashion in Donley County.

Kate laughed in later years at the bedraggled spectacle she must have made when, after a three-day buggy ride from the railhead at Harrold, with two nights spent sleeping out and no change of clothing, she climbed down from her seat beside Bruce in front of the White House. But Mrs. Allen, wife of the hotel's current manager, hastened the next morning to tell the curious women in town that the bride "looked like a queen, my dears, simply like a queen."

The McClelland house, though only a modest frame cottage, was a mansion by comparison with other dwellings in the area, and its gracious furnishings reflected the gentler land that Kate had left behind. In November formal invitations went out to the favored few to attend a housewarming at "Valhalla." But according to western custom, an "open house" meant just that, a general welcome to all, stranger and friend alike, who cared to partake of the host's hospitality. Word of the magnificence of Bruce's house and the beauty of his bride had spread among the settlers, and, just in time to lay on additional refreshments, the young couple learned that all Clarendon planned to come that night. Conversation, music, and improvised entertainments flourished, and, though Kate worried about running out of food, the uninvited guests were never the wiser. The success of the housewarming assured for always the social prestige of the gentlewoman who gave it.

CHAPTER 15

The Conflict of Civilization

(The Railroad and Agriculture)

DURING the 1880's the era of free grass reached its height. With the ranches in the Canadian River region increasing in number, business thrived proportionately, and other merchants moved into Tascosa to compete with Kimball and the Spaniards for the trade of the prospering stockmen. The first to come, as mentioned earlier, were George T. Howard and Ira Rinehart.

Upon the appearance of James E. McMasters the following spring, Howard sold out to Rinehart, and in partnership with the newcomer bought twenty-four acres of land from the surveying firm of Gunter and Munson. There they erected an adobe store in which they stocked every article of trade that could possibly be hauled in from Las Vegas or Dodge City. Soon Jack Ryan, wagon boss of the LX outfit, deserted his job to erect the first saloon. At once the road that ran in front of these two places of business became the main street of the town. Rinehart, determined not to be outdone by his former associate, purchased forty acres directly across the way to establish a rival district. There A. Estlack, who had been an army scout, opened a second saloon, someone else set up a barber shop, Matthew Dunne and his cowboy partner built the town's most imposing drinking place and dance hall, and Bette Trube opened her "eating house."

Very soon both sides of the business block were filled. By the time John Cone and Jim Edwards arrived, they found no available lots close in and were forced to locate about a half-mile east of town on the section owned by Casimero Romero. It was this district that later came to be known as Hog Town. Their long adobe building, previously mentioned, was divided into three parts, a single room, stocked with merchandise and supplies, and close to it a horse corral for the freighters' teams, and a double room which was rented to Jenkins and Donnally for a saloon and dance hall.

In the fall of 1880, Oldham County was organized, and in 1881 Tascosa became the county seat. In that same year the Exchange Hotel was built, and the cowboy capital was well on the way to success.

In March, 1886, there occurred a tragedy characteristic of both the town and the era. It was the outcome of a series of situations peculiar to the cattle country in the days before the establishment of a recognized order—situations that arose from time to time over a period of several years and culminated in the formation of two opposing factions, with the individual stockmen and hands banded against the large operations.

It began with a ruling that employees of certain outfits had to go unarmed and that all outsiders were to be refused the privilege of "working through" at the time of the general roundups—a measure which made it impossible to recover any single animal that had strayed into the larger herds during the winter months. Cattle stealing, always a source of annoyance and material loss and something over which the natural process of law as then administered had little effect, assumed such proportions that rangers were imported as a forceful means of discouraging thievery.

Upon their departure, "fighting men" were hired by many of the outfits to take their place at a wage of one hundred and fifty dollars a month instead of the usual thirty. The regular employees bitterly resented the presence of these outsiders on the grounds that they, the cowboys, were placed through loyalty in the same dangerous situation as the professional fighter and should therefore be rewarded by a recompense equally high. Their concerted demand for an increase in wages became the only cowboy strike on record.

Chilton, Valle, and King, although little more than boys, were fighting men in the employ of the LS Ranch. One night they rode into Tascosa from their camp on the Canadian and went, as was their custom, to the nearest saloon for an evening of relaxation. After several drinks Valle and Chilton settled down to a game of billiards, but King, preferring more convivial amusement, continued his round of the bars, accompanied by John Lang, another LS hand.

Sometime after midnight they happened into the alley just at the time when Lem Woodruff and his friend Emory were locking up for the night. Lem, although employed through the winter months as bartender in Matthew Dunne's saloon, was also joint owner with his boss in a herd of cattle. With the attitude of all small operators, he had little use for any representative of a large outfit, particularly the LS, where he had once worked. And, having himself been a cowboy, he was particularly resentful of the presence anywhere of a professional fighting man.

As Woodruff turned around from the door, King

and Lang recognized the approach of a foe. There was a burst of hot words from both sides, a flash of gunpowder, and King dropped. But, even though mortally wounded, he managed to return his assailant's fire with accuracy. Emory staggered off the street, and Woodruff, more seriously injured, dragged himself to his own room at the rear of the saloon. Lang, having escaped unharmed, hastened to notify Valle and Chilton of the unexpected turn of events. By the time they reached the scene of action, Woodruff was out of sight. Immediately, they laid siege to the door behind which he had taken refuge. Jesse Sheets, owner of an adjoining restaurant, put his head out to learn the cause of the continued bombardment and, being mistaken for an enemy, was picked off. Meanwhile, friends came to the assistance of Woodruff. With their first shot Valle fell, then Chilton, a bullet through his head.

The next afternoon the four murdered men were laid to rest in a cemetery fittingly called Boothill. Every man, woman, and child in the vicinity was present when Judge Wallace, minister ex-officio, administered the last rites by a simple recital of the Twenty-third Psalm. But few tears were shed over the LS boys. In the eyes of the community they were, after all, only interfering strangers who had received their just deserts and whose loss was not

a matter for general mourning. Louis Bozeman and Gough, sometimes called "the Catfish Kid," were accused of the murder of Valle and Chilton, but, like Emory and Woodruff, they were completely exonerated when brought to trial.

On or about June 12, 1886, three months after this sanguinary affair, the first issue of the *Tascosa Pioneer* appeared "to tip its beaver hat to the people of the Panhandle" and the empire of free grass.

Meanwhile Mobeetie had expanded to accommodate a population of seven hundred and fifty. The picket houses and tents of Hidetown and Sweetwater had long since been replaced by more substantial structures of frame and adobe—and a pretty picture they made lying as they did scattered around on the hills above the creek.

The business section of town was concentrated on a few main blocks which ran from east to west. On the north side were Clampett's livery stable and the Huselby Hotel, John Miller's barber shop, Dr. Boyton's drug store, C. L. Pendleton's saloon, Rath Hamberg's mercantile store, another saloon, and F. N. Goodlin's store. Across the street in the next block were Joe Mason's saloon, the "Cattle Exchange," Miller's wagonyard and livery stable, and the Grand Central Hotel, run by Thomas O'Laughlin and his wife. Next was the corral for the freighters' ox-teams, an entire block fenced in with pickets, with a camp house and beer saloon inside as an accommodation for the men.

Opposite, going in the other direction, the establishment of Cindy Carter, the old black woman who did the entire town's laundry came first; then came the hardware store of McKinney and Huffman, which occupied a building owned by Major Van Horn from Dodge City, whom Morris Rosenfield had forced from business in Clarendon; Johnny Long's saloon, the "Mint," which was next, proved to be all that the name implied; beside it was a gambling hall, then another saloon. In fact, almost every other business house was for the purpose of dispensing liquor. John L. and Wiley Dickerson had a general store, with Tom Riley's saloon on the corner next to them, then C. L. Bennet's barbershop, and another drinking emporium called the "Palace" and run by Bert Clampett. The law office of Grigsby and Houston was close by, and Mr. and Mrs. Boles's drygoods store, Brown's ready-to-wear, and another livery stable completed the business section.

Living in town were several families: Judge Woodman and his pretty, slender, redheaded wife, Judge Browning, and Judge Patton and his wife, who had come near to being killed in bed by a band of drunken cowboys who playfully "shot up the town" one night. Temple Houston, the Raven's son, and the southern aristocrat he married were a familiar sight, especially in the early evening when it was their custom to walk hand in hand from one end to the other of the veranda running the length of their frame cottage. On nearby ranches were Ben Masterson and Robert Hamilton, owners of the Long S, Nick Eaton, who branded U-U, and Hank Creswell, whose cattle wore a Bar CC.

School was conducted in an upstairs room of the rock courthouse with one teacher supplying all the grades. Church services were held wherever convenient.

On the north edge of town was the restricted district known as "Feather Hill." Of its many occupants the most notorious was Ella, the "Diamond Girl," so called because, contrary to the habits of her sisters in the profession who attired themselves in "Mother Hubbards," she never appeared in public unless gowned in black satin, with diamonds glistening from every wearable place. Her romantic story is one of the town's best known legends, possibly because the boy she loved was a young lieutenant from the fort and the suitor who killed her a cowpuncher from a nearby ranch.

In the Donley region, Clarendon, too, was at the pinnacle of success. Its only rivals were Tascosa and Mobeetie, all flourishing in like manner upon free grass. But, without the neutralizing force of easy transportation, the one was too far away to offer serious competition, and the other was chiefly a reflection of the glory cast by the former presence of Fort Elliott and the law. The era of the soldier was past, and, upon the organization of Donley County, Clarendon took equal rank with Mobeetie as a seat of local government. The herd of the Quarter Circle Heart outfit totaled over thirty-five thousand head, and the colony boasted a population of three hundred. But progress operates in cycles, each one of which, according to the geometric law, describes its arc by moving from a given point of beginning up and around and then *down* to a plainly defined point of end.

During February of 1885 work had been resumed on the Fort Worth and Denver Railroad. As each additional tie brought the railroad closer to the little town at the foot of the cap rock, tent settlements sprang up all along the way in advance of its track. Eagle Flat had become Vernon and under its new name was made the county seat of Wilbarger. J. V. Johnson commenced the box house around which Quanah was to grow. On September 15, 1886, the *Tascosa Pioneer* stated that the Ft.

Worth and Denver would extend "to the Canadian, almost two hundred miles from Harrold. The road is now graded [almost to the Red River] and, when track laying begins, it will be pushed very rapidly."

At about the same time the Southern Kansas Railroad announced its intention of bisecting the plains in a horizontal direction. When completed, the surveys of the two roads showed a junction at Carson City with the proposed track of the former crossing the Salt Fork within a mile of Clarendon, at a place where the rock formation of the earth offered an excellent foundation for the bridge necessary to span the river. It then proceeded over the divide lying between the Carroll and Allen creeks to the high level country beyond the cap rock. But before it was too late, one of the Dyer boys called attention to the mistake made by the engineers in overlooking the one place in the Panhandle where the ascent from prairie to plain was gradual and unbroken by riverbed or canyon. A hurried investigation proved Dyer's assertion correct and resulted in a second survey that charted a route far to the west of the original course, missing Carson City, the colony, and Tascosa and Mobeetie by many miles, and pronouncing the final doom of the last three places.

As soon as the new point of junction became a matter of certainty, Colonel Berry, firm in his belief that its location would determine the location of Northwest Texas' chief metropolis, looked up the number of the section, filed on the land, and with the assistance of the Fort Worth and Denver agent, laid out a townsite, which he called "Oneida." The Old Town Land Company was then organized by Judge Wallace, Williams Martin, C. W. Martin, J. J. Meadors, C. W. Merchant, John Hollicott, and W. W. Westell, for the purpose of promoting the new town.

On August 30, 1887, an election was held to select the county seat of the newly organized county of Potter, with fifty-three voters casting their ballots at the headquarters of the LX and Frying Pan ranches. In September, Judge McMasters of Tascosa, where the counting was done, wrote into the minutes of the court that a majority of forty-five votes had been cast in favor of Berry's city, but he failed to include in his report that most of the voters were cowboys who had been promised by the promoter two townsite lots each if the election results were favorable.

Because the sandy bed of a nearby creek was the color of gold, the original name was soon discarded for the more appropriate one of Amarilla, correctly pronounced "A-ma-re-ya" until changed to its present masculine form Amarillo and Anglicized.

Most of the town's officials were cowboys and unmarried. The courthouse cost only a hundred and fifty dollars but was, nevertheless, the regional center where all marriages were performed, all trades were made, and innumerable yarns were swapped in the days before the county completed its pretentious $33,000 building on the edge of the creek. School was held in a boxlike room with a dirt floor, located so close to a lake that during rainy spells classes had to be dismissed. The little cemetery called "Llano" lay across the line in the next county, and the butcher kept as pets a "loafer" wolf and her two pups called Sullivan and Kilrain, which, while tied to a post in front of the shop, furnished music until dawn for the guests of the nearby Tremont Hotel. As there was no minister, Judge H. H. Wallace, who had moved down from Tascosa, officiated at marriage ceremonies—with the assistance of only an Episcopal prayer book.

The newspaper was called the *Champion* and was edited by a firebrand named Brooks. The town boasted twelve hundred inhabitants, and the majority of them still lived in tents. Notwithstanding these primitive conditions, it was at one time the biggest shipping point for cattle the United States had ever known.

But as shrewd as Berry had been in founding Oneida, there was one important factor in its development that he overlooked. The railroad, upon which its success depended, cut the Frying Pan Ranch almost in half. This tract of 250,000 acres was owned by J. F. Glidden and H. B. Sanborn, the former the imaginative tinkerer who saw a fortune in staples hanging loose on a fence, and the latter the Yankee drummer who, having sold the idea to Texas, proceeded to enclose Northwest Texas in barbed wire.[1] As the county seat boomed, the erstwhile salesman decided it would be advantageous to move it out of the draw onto higher land a mile away, which he happened to own. So Sanborn set to work to accomplish through ingenuity and perseverance his desired purpose. By various subtle means of persuasion, such as the construction of a $50,000 hotel that totally eclipsed the courthouse in grandeur, he managed, so to speak, to put the old town on wheels and roll it over to the site of his preference, where Amarillo stands today.

With Amarillo's establishment began the age of agriculture and industry. In spite of the fact that it once held

the record as a cattle shipping point and is at present the only city of any size in the part of Texas known as the cattleman's country, Amarillo is not now and never was a typical "cow town." It owes its birth to the railroad and the Yankee and its life to wheat and oil. Its purpose was in accord with the advance of the era. Therefore it is the only one of the frontier settlements that has truly survived the test of time to become a fast-growing metropolis.

In the fall of 1886, a committee of Fort Worth and Denver officials and other citizens met at the courthouse to discuss plans for the new Clarendon. The railroad promised to build roundhouses and make a division point of the town provided the land necessary for the project was made available to them without cost—a proposition to which the people consented with the understanding that four hundred lots would be set aside for the personal use of those desirous of changing their place of residence. The location agreed on was a section near a small lake, five miles to the south of the Salt Fork. It was the property of J. C. Phillips. Some slight difficulty was encountered in persuading him to sell anything for the benefit of a "lot of damn Yankees," as he called the railroad men, but his friend "Rosie" (Morris Rosenfield) finally convinced

[1] Sanborn, the man who introduced barbed wire, was born in New York and went west to seek his fortune. Arriving in DeKalb, Illinois, in 1854, he lived with J. F. Glidden, who invented barbed wire. As Glidden's agent, Sanborn sold his first ten reels of wire at Gainesville, Texas, in 1875 (B. B. Paddock, ed., *A Twentieth Century History and Biographical Record of North and West Texas*, I, 302).

him that it was the proper course to follow, and the deal was closed. Swiftly, the day of the open range was drawing to a close.

However, the outset of the frontier cowman's difficulties antedated the end of the colony by many years. As the absorption of the public domain slowly progressed, the primitive custom of dividing properties by such natural means as streams and arroyos and ridges was generally replaced by the more formal system of fencing.[2] The resulting transition from open to enclosed ownership necessitated a revolutionary change in the method of handling cattle; unfortunately, many old-timers were never able to adapt to the new ways. For instance, when the instinctive movements of the herds were restrained by artificial barriers and the animals were no longer able to shift from one vantage point to another according to the dictates of hunger, thirst, or temperature, man-conceived measures of protection had to be devised.

[2] According to Harley True Burton, *A History of the J. A. Ranch*, p. 93, "The first wire fence was built by Henry Taylor and Bill Koogle on the J. A. Ranch in 1882. It was what is known as a drift fence. . . . [It] extended along the northern part of the ranch and was built (very characteristic of Goodnight) more to keep the other ranchmen's cattle from drifting in from the North (and grazing on the J. A. range) than to keep the Goodnight cattle from drifting."

From the first there existed an open antagonism between stockman and farmer. The man whose cattle grazed the open range was, like the Indian, firm in the belief that "the earth . . . is our mother and her body should not be disturbed by hoe or plow. Man should subsist by the spontaneous production of Nature. The sovereignty of the earth cannot be sold or given away."[3] This determined conviction of the cowman that the country belonged only to him and his kind did not offer much encouragement to new settlers. Consequently, many of the earliest farmers were men of undesirable quality, "nesters" whose presence contributed nothing toward the region's development and added materially to the woes of those already in possession, particularly as the checkerboard system of alternate school and railroad grants placed them on scattered sections all over the holdings of the ranching outfits, to the great disadvantage of both factions. Sometimes the big operator was forced to buy out the intruder at an exorbitant price, but more often the weaker individual was coerced into submission by fencing in or fencing out or, on occasion, less lawful measures.

However, the antagonism lay much deeper than a

[3] From a speech made by Too-hul-hul-sote of the Nez Perce, quoted in Mathew W. Stirling, "America's First Settlers, the Indians," *National Geographic* 72 (November 1937), 575.

mere struggle for possession of the land. It was the spiritual conflict of opposing cultures; the one evolved from a gentle background of forest and stream, security, central government, recognized traditions and plodding ways, the other from the freedom of spaces, the power and pride of fleet horses, spectacular gestures, and men armed with guns. Much experience and understanding was necessary before either could come to sympathize with the other's needs or the two could live in harmony.

Soon the controversy had extended into the broader field of politics, with the merchants in the populated areas actively on the side of the farmer because increased settlement meant increased trade for them. Not only was the Panhandle divided against itself, but the entire eastern part of the state was solid in its opposition to the western part and the interest of cattle. As early as 1879, the legislators succeeded in passing the first of many laws formulated as preventive measures and as inducements to settling.[4] This law permitted grazing land to be sold in quantities up to three sections. In 1881, an amendment known colloquially as the "Seven Section Act" was added, permitting the sale of seven sections of grazing land five miles outside of the geographic center of any county.[5]

During these early years of the 1880's, the free grass era was moving rapidly toward its peak. Untold thousands of cattle grazed and fattened without payment upon public land as yet unsurveyed or filed on. In an attempt to thwart the use of free grass, the Sales Act of 1883 created a state land board and empowered it to lease common school, university, and asylum lands for terms up to ten years at an annual rental of four cents per acre.[6]

Because both the land board and the lease laws continued to be held in low esteem, the state land board issued its Resolution No. 8 of February 27, 1884, providing higher minimum rent and shorter terms of lease and stating that "prices shall be eight cents per acre per year and lease periods of no longer than six years."[7]

[4] H. P. N. Gammel, comp., *Laws of Texas*, IX, 391 (courtesy Sam J. Dealey of the Dallas firm of Jackson, Walker, Winstead, Cantwell, and Miller).
[5] Sales Act of 1881 (5), as amended (ibid., p. 212).
[6] Ibid.
[7] Ibid.

By this time, the more intelligent stockmen were beginning to realize that the farmer had come to stay and that the payment of lease might be the lesser of two evils. Goodnight and many others were of the opinion that free grass and lawlessness were one and the same and that a more stable system of holding land might bring greater prosperity to the cattleman—that is, if the lease price was fair. But, between the politician's and the Westerner's conception of the word "fair" lay a wide difference of opinion. Eight cents was an exorbitant price that even those in favor of leasing had not the slightest intention of paying. In the beginning, leasing had been put upon a competitive basis, but, through mutual agreement, no cowman ever bid against another, and the four-cent minimum was all that was ever paid. While this may have complied with the letter of the law, it did not meet its spirit. After another twelve months, in a last desperate effort to force their point, the legislature passed the Land Fraud Act, making it a misdemeanor to appropriate public land without proper payment. By this possibly unavoidable but nevertheless unfortunate choice of term, the law-makers themselves became accomplices to the miscarriage of justice and created one of the most ludicrous situations in the history of Northwest Texas.

A misdemeanor, according to legal procedure, can be

tried only under the judicial body of the district in which the offense so termed is committed. Imagine—a cowman on trial for evasion of a law conceived in direct opposition to his own interests and to those of the majority of the people of the community in which the procedure was conducted, the legal body formed of men of sympathetic outlook, and the jury composed of boys from his own or neighboring outfits. As a result, any person so accused was immediately cleared "by trial" or "for written reasons by the county attorney."

By January, 1886,[8] indictments had been returned against every cattleman in the Donley district, including Goodnight. However, their trials were not held until the court session of the following summer. This was so important a matter that Attorney General Templeton himself made the long journey up from Austin to see that, for once, justice was served in a Clarendon colony court. But even the presence of so august a representative of the law had small effect on the Western system. Case followed case without a single conviction.

At last, Willis, the presiding judge, wearied by the endless travesty being enacted before him, arose to announce his intention of throwing the remaining cases out of court, citing as his reason the fact that every one on the docket was of a nature so similar to those that had gone before that acquittal was certain; therefore, he saw no need or advantage in wasting further the state's funds.

Jumping to his feet, the chagrined and infuriated Templeton shouted, "I'll have you impeached for this." But it was two years before the impeachment proceedings were instituted, and by that time Templeton had been succeeded as attorney general by Jim Hogg. When the case came to trial in Austin, many prominent men from the Panhandle were called as witnesses and the ablest lawyers in Texas were engaged for the defense, among them the firm of Walton, Hill and Walton of Austin, Judge Carroll from Denton, and "Cyclone" Davis from Kaufman. From beginning to end, the issue centered around the trial of Goodnight; the prosecution's two chief insinuations were that a jury composed of cowboys and of citizens of a community to which the accused man had made such generous contributions could not help being prejudiced and that not only had Willis been cognizant of this fact, but he was a party to it, as proved by his final actions.

After days of argument, the judge arose in his own defense and, in the slow, drawling tone so characteristic of him, made to a jury composed of state senators a masterful plea that ended:

8 The grand jury convened in late December, 1885, but there was no court session until the following month, January, 1886.

Before God and man I say to this Honorable Senate that I ask no pity and seek no mercy, but I do ask acquittal under the principal of calm and cold law and facts in this case. In the name of the law of the land, I demand that this stain on my reputation be wiped out by not only an acquittal but a complete vindication. If I had refused to try the case, ignoring the law in the case, then I would have been accused of collusion with a large ranch man to liberate him without trial and to defraud the state of a trial of the issue and of the rental value of the school land, and of letting the criminal go free by my own judgment instead of leaving it to the jury. It is true that Goodnight's men were on the jury, because Donley County was practically unpopulated except by Goodnight and his employees, hence there were so few men in that county to qualify for jury service that the county officers were forced to take some of Goodnight's men, or else there could have been no jury at all. Now when I came to the trial, what should I do? I defy this honorable body and the law officers of the state to show me some law that would have authorized me to prorogue and dismiss those juries as a dictator, to step off the bench and issue an ukase depriving the county of a term of court which the law said that they should have. This prosecution is placed in part upon one charge that these land fraud cases should not have been tried in Donley County at all, which charge is a misconception of the law of Texas since there is no way on earth by which a misdemeanor case can be removed from the county in which it is instituted or where its venue belongs, even though the defendant should consent thereto, since there is fundamentally no jurisdiction in any other county other than the one where the charge is preferred, and there was no venue in another county than Donley.

I dislike to refer to the insinuation that the building and donation of a church by Goodnight was a species of bribery. Now sirs, let me ask the fair-minded men in this Honorable Body when it has become wrong in public-spirited men, philanthropists, and good people to build a church for the glory of God and salvation of men? Now in the presence of God and this Honorable Body I declare that "Thus saith the Law" governed me in every action I took and the environment under which I worked and sparse population of the county left me no other course than the one I did pursue.[9]

The senate voted and by a majority of twenty to five favored acquittal. When Judge Willis reached Clarendon on his return after being exonerated, he was greeted by the firing of anvils and the ringing of the bell as a

[9] Judge Newton P. Willis, son of Judge Frank Willis, affirmed that "To the best of my knowledge, my father's speech was as [quoted here]" (author's interview with Judge Newton P. Willis, August 16, 1936, Lewis Papers, Archives, Dallas Histrical Society).

manifestation of the citizens' feeling toward him. His ride home from the colony was doubtless the wildest in his career. The stage on which he traveled was not due at Mobeetie till sundown, but Roxy, the driver, having been requested to speed his schedule by an hour, if possible, applied the whip with steady perseverance and stopped for nothing. A few miles out from town twenty-five cowboys rode up, delaying progress long enough to tie on with their lariats and to pass the bottle of welcome for a few rounds. When the journey was resumed, it was to the accompaniment of drunken shouts and the clatter of horses' hoofs as the stage hurtled forward on the heels of the terrified mules. The heads of its inmates all but burst through the top with each successive jolt.

On the outskirts of Mobeetie, a more orderly delegation awaited in more somber vehicles, among which was an ambulance borrowed from the fort, the only equipage available with the dignity suitable to the occasion. Thus, seated behind hospital insignia and escorted by the local band, Judge Willis made his triumphant entry into town. The musicians afterward boasted that, although most of them were too drunk to stand without leaning one against the other, not a note was missed. All of the many saloons opened their doors extra wide, torches burned, banners flew, and there was truly a "hot time in the old town" that night.

Sometime later, another lease law went into effect, again permitting leasing at four cents an acre and for a term of five years.[10] Goodnight was largely responsible for its passing. He was shrewd enough to see the trend of the times and to know that with a five-year lease at so nominal a sum he had legally extended free grass for himself for a few years anyway.

The sentiment in the free grass district was loud against him, as is shown by the following editorial from the *Tascosa Pioneer*, December 10, 1887:

> The life of Charles Goodnight is being written by a Clarendon gentleman. It ought to make decidedly interesting reading and furnish some uncommonly juicy developments. No doubt it will be illustrated with some suggestive and beautiful scenes. It is presumed that the frontispiece will show a distinguished-looking baron in the middle of a barbed-wire empire. In the background you will notice numerous partition fences, in each enclosure exactly twenty acres, and grazing thereon one steer. Various "Notices to the Public" will be observed fluttering in sight promiscuously, warning all trespassers

[10] Sales Act of 1887, in Gammel, *Laws of Texas*, IX, 882.

that this domain is held by right of four cents per acre lease, and an absolute relinquishment by the state for that mammoth consideration for a period of five years. A crowd of discouraged looking "actual settlers" will be seen drawing out and away from their claims "which are really not worth anything," induced to go because "crops" failed and because it wasn't very comfortable anyway. Inspection will show that the baron is mounted, and his mount can be seen to be a burro, the longest eared and heaviest browed and thickest skulled breed with the "State of Texas" in green letters (color of children's grass) on his lean side. To one side the ground will be covered with a mangled and defunct corporation, the late lamented land board. From the side pocket of the baron will protrude (that is, we are speaking of what should be) a small corner of the thirty-third judicial district, evidently the receptacle for his lordship's proboscis. The plain inference of the entire volume will be confirmed in the summing up: the conclusion of the matter will be that the "Panhandle is not fit for agriculture and not very good for grazing." The moral: who blames a man for riding even a donkey when the donkey is anxious to be ridden—and it pays?

It is difficult to know how much of the above was inspired by a difference of political views and how much by antagonism toward the man himself. Concerning Goodnight there was no halfway ground to feeling. To one and all he was either the god of the West who made the Panhandle or the scoundrel who in every way retarded its progress.

As a matter of fact, he was neither, but was, instead, an uncompromising individualist whose only interest was cattle and who believed that when the farmer came, the cow would go; he was little concerned with the development of the country other than as it affected his personal interests, but withal he was a shrewd if almost illiterate frontiersman who realized then what the following half-century helped to prove—that a land, however fertile, if low in rainfall, lacking in water, and erratic in climate, is primarily a grazing country where "the farmer by hard work may do better some seasons than a living, but cannot get rich and only continues to do well when he combines crop-planting with stock-raising."[11]

[11] J. Evetts Haley, *Charles Goodnight, Cowman and Plainsman*, p. 383.

CHAPTER 16

Conclusion

(The Passing of the Frontier)

THE trial of Willis took place in 1887, the first major event of the memorable year that brought to an end the most romantic period in the history of the Panhandle. Some months before, the *Tascosa Pioneer* had made the assertion that "Free Grass is no more for Texas, and, in the West, politicians and home-hunters have 'done' for cattle." But there were contributing factors besides those connected with politics—the advance of agriculture and the coming of the railroad—one national, the other regional.

The cattle industry all over America was suffering a decline as the result of growing competition and glutted markets. In Northwest Texas overcrowding herds had so reduced the grass of the range that any unusual atmospheric condition was certain to bring disaster. The weather had favored the stockman during the early 1880's. Each spring the rains had fallen, and mild winters had followed seasons of plenty. But the end was at hand. Long-suffering nature stood ready to strike back in all her fury at the unwelcome strangers who fed so avidly upon her bounty.

The summer of 1886 witnessed the worst drouth on record; the following year opened with a blizzard so severe that old-timers still claim the gulf froze over—a natural sequence in a region where one climatic extreme invariably accompanies another. The gulf story may be an exaggeration, but the freeze was, in fact, a catastrophe that exterminated countless herds and hastened materially the failure of the first big company.

When the Francklyn Company went into the hands of the receiver after having been foreclosed upon by a specific class of English lienholders, the *Tascosa Pioneer* reported the affair on September 1, 1886, as follows:

> The collapse of . . . one of the most prominent corporations in the Panhandle . . . , controlling ranges that aggregated hundreds of thousands of acres and with an ownership of some fifty thousand head of stock . . . is an item of unusual interest. The papers issued by [the new manager], who had been sent by the New York creditors of the company to investigate its range affairs, show [that] out of a herd of fifty-six thousand head, less fourteen thousand sold, . . . only about four and a

half thousand can be accounted for. The cattle were wasted, scattered and lost and debts confront a stockless and broke corporation. How far this fearful mismanagement was a swindle no one knows.

Gradually many of the other large companies went the way of the Francklyn, and many more, having foreseen the trend of the times, averted disaster by dividing up or changing hands just before the impending crash materialized. Of the numerous onetime flourishing outfits, only a few survive with the original brand and most of their original holdings, among them the Spade Ranch, the Pitchfork, and the Matador.[1]

In June, 1887, Count Kearney arrived from abroad to investigate the dubious affairs of the Clarendon Land Investment and Agency Company. For some time dissatisfaction had been increasing among the stockholders, particularly among the class who had never received a dividend. The consensus was that ranch and land project alike were being handled only for the advantage of the American investors. Upon being told by Charlie O'Donel, Kearney's nephew who had been with the outfit for some time, that the English executives would arrive on a certain day, both Lewis Henry Carhart and Al McKinney

[1] The author is not certain whether this is still correct.

resigned without the formality of notice and departed from town.

A tour of inspection showed conditions worse even than Kearney had anticipated; the herd counted only a fraction of its supposed number, and other signs of gross mismanagement were present on all sides. Realizing that only by drastic measures could he salvage anything from the wreck for his clients, the Britisher set to work immediately to reorganize. Henry Taylor was installed as range boss, and O'Donel took the minister's place as manager. Thus ended the Clarendon Land Investment and Agency Company. Today, on the range where once grazed the thirty-five thousand cattle that formed the Quarter Circle Heart herd, there are farms and country school grounds and crossroads settlements—and one of the frontier's most ambitious ventures is only a romantic tale of times long past.

Three months after the arrival of Kearney, the Fort Worth and Denver reached the new town. On September 9, the gold spike connecting the local division with the main road was driven in. Every well-known man in the county took part in the ceremony and the barbecue that followed.

On Tuesday, November 12, the first passenger run was made to the switch below town. The people went wild when the big engine with its bright red wheels came into view. Within a few days a tent city had sprung up by the side of the newly laid tracks. Strange faces and strange people were everywhere. The name was unchanged, but that was all.

With the coming of the railroad and a new era, a new Clarendon emerged. A few families and a few houses remained still on the flat across the river, but the Christian colony was no more.

Carhart returned at once to active work in the church but for many reasons was never able to pick up the scattered threads of his former life. In 1891 he resigned and moved to Hot Springs, Arkansas, to invest all that remained of his fortune—about ten thousand dollars—in a bath-house. From there he drifted on to California, where he died, a forgotten and disillusioned old man in the Union Solders' Home at Sawtelle.

In 1885, Adair had died in St. Louis on his way home from a third trip to the JA Ranch, after which Goodnight felt that with the conditions in the industry as they were, a dissolution of partnership at the expiration of the contract would best serve the interests of himself and the Irishman's widow and heir.

When the time of property division arrived, he took the Quitaque Ranch with its 140,000 acres and twenty thousand head of cattle, leaving Mrs. Adair in possession of the remainder, together with the brand he had made famous. "On December 27, 1887, he left the Palo Duro, the creation of his own genius, the product of his labor, and the object of his dearest affections to move over on the railroad and settle at the station called in his honor."[2]

This move was the catastrophe that closed a tragic year—the initial step in the downfall of the Panhandle's first cowman and the greatest baron produced by the free grass era. From beginning to end, he was a frontiersman in attitude as well as practice—a perfect example of the person who succeeds because he is in accord with his time and who, for the same reason, fails when he lives beyond it. Before death ended his career at the age of ninety-three, he had long since ceased to be a figure of importance and was merely another impoverished and defeated old man— a pitiable and feeble reminder of the lusty period he represented.

Many years have elapsed since the days when Goodnight was lord of the plains, and little remains of all that was once his West. Mobeetie is now a combination of the old and new towns. With the coming of the railroad,

[2] J. Evetts Haley, *Charles Goodnight, Cowman and Plainsman*, p. 333.

most of the inhabitants of the original town moved to a location sometimes called "New Town" near the newly laid tracks of the Panhandle and Santa Fe Railroad. The old Mobeetie is only a small settlement of houses and stores. A short distance away, a marker under the heading of "O. F. E." reads: "This is the old Fort Elliott Reservation, established 1874, abandoned 1891—named in honor of the early days."

Tascosa, the wild and lawless capital of free grass, is no more. By the early part of the twentieth century it had already become a ghost town. In 1939, when Cal Farley founded his Boys' Ranch for homeless and unfortunate boys, there remained of the old town only its courthouse and its cemetery. The courthouse was first used as a home for the boys, but it has now become the Julian Bivins Museum and contains the awards and mementoes of Mr. Farley's career and many artifacts and items reminiscent of the days when Tascosa was an important community of the Old West.

The waters of a large government dam cover the land on which the Clarendon colony was once located. Although a new hospital and a new junior college have been erected, the present Clarendon lacks the leadership and distinction of its earlier years. Buses and motor cars have replaced the Fort Worth and Denver trains, and life is the uneventful life of a small town.

Railroads, wheat fields, and oil derricks are now commonplace in the Panhandle. All the large ranches have been reduced either by a sale of parts or by division among heirs. In spite of this, cattle by the thousands still graze the grasses of the Texas Northwest, and the cowboy remains the region's dominant figure. Unfortunately, he is no longer the Southern boy who has gone west to escape the ravages of a civil war. Nor is he a drifter or a professional gunman. He is more often than not a nester's son who has grown up near a ranch. He has only the mannerisms, not the true manner of the revered "old-timer."

The Panhandle and its people have undergone great changes in modern times. It is no longer an isolated little kingdom of its own, but an integral part of the great outside world. The land itself, however, remains as it was in the beginning—a highly fertile, semi-arid region with a scarcity of water, where the cowboy, be he nester or otherwise, his mount a pickup or a pony, may once again rule supreme.

Additional Facts, Figures, and Stories

DOAN'S STORE

THE trail-driving era began during the last years of the Civil War when an enterprising and hard-pressed Texan conceived the idea of gathering a small bunch from the thousands of cattle roaming wild between the Nueces River and the Rio Grande and driving them to market in New Orleans.[1] By 1870, his idea of gathering wild cattle and trailing them to market had become a practice both widespread and lucrative but cattlemen by then looked to northern markets. The first trail north was established by one Jesse Chisholm, said by some to be half-Indian, who drove his cattle through the Indian Territory before and during the war, "crossing the Red River at Choke Bluff Crossing below Denison."[2] It was this Chisholm Trail which later became the well-known Eastern Trail. As both settlement and the size and number of the herds increased, it became necessary to form a link farther to the west. It was on this so-called Western Trail that in later years the largest herds were trailed, herds driven by men with such famous names as Ab and John Blocker, D. R. Fant, J. F. Glidden (who invented barbed wire), John Lytte, Noah Ellis, Ephraim Harrold, William Ikard, Worsham, Belcher, Legon, Clerk, Wiley Blair, Eddlemans, and Dubose. Both trails started out from San Antonio, then converged at Fort Griffin to separate again, the one proceeding to Kansas through the Indian Territory and the other to Dodge City, crossing the Red River at Doan's store.

Located a short distance below the river, Doan's is not an integral part of Panhandle history but it is included here because it was trail driving that focused the eyes of America and England on Northwest Texas.

During the early 1870's, Jonathan Doan was living in Kansas where, assisted by his nephew Corvin and under government protection, he trafficked with the

[1] J. Frank Dobie, *The Longhorns*, p. 11.

[2] C. H. Rust, quoted in George W. Saunders, ed., *The Trail Drivers of Texas*, p. 40.

Indians in furs and pelts. Upon the death of his wife, Jonathan decided to move to Texas. After getting permission from the authorities at Fort Sill to open a store within the stockade, he moved to the Indian Territory, accompanied by Corvin, his sister Phoebe, and his two motherless daughters.

Business was brisk, and all went well until Jonathan decided to return to the nomadic life he had enjoyed before his marriage. Corvin was left in sole charge of both the business and the family. After a short period, the threat of an Indian uprising and the sudden death of Phoebe persuaded him to relinquish the store and to return with the girls to his old home in Ohio. Meanwhile, Jonathan was traveling over the Panhandle in a covered wagon stocked with merchandise. As time went on, his trade with the buffalo hunters grew to such proportions that he considered it necessary to establish supply camps, first on Buck Creek, then on Wanderer's Creek, and finally on a creek a mile and a half from the Prairie Dog Fork of the Red River at a place the Indians called Toso Padachopie, which in their language means Elm Springs.[3]

It is the last-named supply depot that forms the theme of this story. Business flourished, and soon all

[3] Now called Doans. See map of Wilbarger County, *Texas Almanac, 1966–1967*, p. 328.

Jonathan's attention was given to Elm Springs. Extravagant reports of the beauty of the surroundings and the successful trade went to Ohio.

During this short period, Corvin had married and settled down. However, he had never quite relinquished the hope that some day he would return to the Southwest. Jonathan's letters were all that was needed to bring about a quick decision. Some delay was caused by the birth of a baby daughter, but soon all was in readiness for the long move, and the party was on its way. Besides his wife, Lide, and the newborn infant, Corvin was accompanied by Jonathan's two daughters and an uncle, Cal W. Doan.

On September 25, 1878, they left Sherman, Texas, the railroad terminus, to make the rest of the journey overland in wagons driven by freighters familiar with Jonathan and his camp at Elm Springs. When the destination was finally reached, the travel-worn family was little prepared to meet the situation they found facing them. Instead of the busy store so graphically described by Jonathan, there was a deserted picket house with neither stove nor fireplace, stocked with one lone jar of stale mustard, a keg of powder, and large quantities of strychnine. Jonathan was absent, supposedly attending to business elsewhere, and the nearest white neighbors, so the freighters said, lived fifty miles away. In Corvin's pocket was one silver dollar, and dependent upon him were a wife, a babe in arms, an old man, and two girls, seventeen and fifteen years of age. But if he was discouraged, he gave no visible signs as he set to work to make the quarters as livable as possible and to find some immediate source of income.

The picket house was a structure about twenty-four by thirty feet, roofed with grass and mud. At the openings that served as doors and windows, buffalo hides were hung. Skins also made a partition between the family's quarters and the portion reserved for the store.

While the men with the freighters' assistance hastily constructed a stone fireplace, Lide and the girls gathered prairie grasses to fill the mattress ticks. As the floors were dirt, a large box with a carpet in the bottom was rigged up to hold the baby; there, while her mother worked, the infant Bertha taught herself to walk as she went round and round the sides in a never-ceasing effort to get out. The place nearest the fire was always reserved for her, as "the little one must be kept warm at any cost"; on bitter nights this custom caused everyone to clamor to hold her so as to occupy the only comfortable spot in the drafty house.

As soon as the affairs of the household were in order, Corvin turned his attention to the more serious matter of discovering through means close at hand a way to make possible the purchase of merchandise for the prospective store. With an optimism natural in one of his years and especially characteristic of the true pioneer, he had unlimited faith in his own ability and in the success of the ultimate outcome. He expended no part of his vitality— an asset so precious on the frontier—on futile conjectures concerning the future, but lived each hour as it came, accepting, as a matter of course, the bad along with the good.

The surrounding country abounded with animal life. He was an excellent shot, and there were gunpowder and strychnine in plenty. A paying job lay within easy reach. Day by day, he tramped the prairie with his gun or pulled his "drag" along the line over which he scattered poisoned snares.

By spring a high and tidy stock of pelts had been gathered. The check returned by the St. Louis furriers who received them was ample to pay for the first shipment of supplies. The order was placed and preparations hastened that the store might be fully organized and running by early April when the first herds would begin to trail by.

Jonathan, who had not been seen all winter, put in

an unexpected appearance simultaneously with the arrival of the merchandise. For some unknown reason, possibly embarrassment over his unexplained absence, he made no claim of ownership to the new store but asked only to become a partner.

Although the Doans were isolated from civilization, the years that followed were happy ones for all concerned. Corvin, always the dominant spirit, was one of those rare "fortunates" who possess within themselves endless resources, independent of exterior circumstances or surroundings. As soon as possible, he sent back for his library and cornet. After supper when everyone's chores were done, the family gathered in front of the blazing hearth. While Lide quietly plied her needle and Uncle Cal dozed, Corvin made music, or Jonathan, when awake, furnished entertainment by recounting with fitting histrionics absurdly wild tales of his days on the Kansas frontier. Sometimes Corvin read aloud from Dickens, Scott, or the poets of whom he was particularly fond. At holiday times, he sent to Paris for the special edition of *Le Figaro* and to London for the *Graphic*. The girls, as part of their education, were taught to recite verses from these, and almost before she could talk intelligibly, the baby was able to lisp snatches from "Tam-O-Shanter" that she, herself, had picked up as she sat night after night on her father's knee, listening to the lulling words of Burns's poetry.

Often friendly Indians or buffalo hunters stopped overnight to take advantage of the hospitality of the house, and cowboys came from a great distance because they "heard there were some women folks in the neighborhood and, as they hadn't seen a woman for quite a spell, just thought they'd ride over and take a look." Sometimes there were more distinguished guests, such as Uncle George MacTaylor, who had been a major under General Crook in the days when Bill Cody was his army scout, and Mrs. Brown, who came from New York to charm the children with her modish silk frocks and the watch she wore pinned to her shoulder by a jeweled fleur-de-lys. But the favorite of all was the young "saddle-bag" preacher who, although terrified of Indian and cowboy alike, never relinquished his efforts to convert to "a life of eternal peace" the redskins and equally indifferent plainsmen among whom he worked, according to the dictates of conscience.

Across the river in the Territory, not more than a mile distant, camped the Comanches and Kiowas. Of these, Lide, like the little minister, never quite lost her fear. But the girls accepted their dark neighbors as a natural part of their surroundings, played with the children, learned to speak Comanche as fluently as English, and took many rides across the prairies seated bareback behind the fat old squaws. The braves came frequently to the settlement to trade or to seek respite from painful wounds at the hands of the "gentle, white lady."

From his first days on the frontier, Corvin had friendly feelings for and much sympathy toward the Indians. They sensed this, and a good relationship between the white man and the redskins developed. While at Fort Sill, he had often given candy and crackers to the poor squaws and children who nearly starved between governmental issue days. And when Santa Ana and his band decided to exterminate all the whites in the neighborhood, Corvin was forewarned by the Indians. Consequently, Corvin had come to believe firmly that "no Indian would lay hands on a Doan." Only once was his faith somewhat shaken. The incident occurred, as was to be expected, at a time when the women were at home alone. The master of the house was off for the day hunting, and Jonathan and the other men were away on a freighting trip to Fort Worth.

It was a bright spring morning, and Lide, unaware of impending danger, peacefully pursued her usual routine. As she hurried from one task to the next, she happened in passing to glance through the door toward the creek where she had sent the children to gather wood and cowchips for the stove. Only one glimpse of the scene on the horizon before her was necessary to bring her to a sudden stop. Upon the crest of the farthest slope beyond the stream moved an Indian rider, and ahead of him, disappearing from view on the other side, went the last of the few horses left behind by the men.

As she watched, there flashed across her memory an episode of some days past, one to which she had paid little heed at the time. Two boys from downstate had stopped overnight on their way to Kansas. She could still see them as they made ready to leave after breakfast, fearless and gay and transported with the excitement of their adventure. They had already reached the cattle highway when Corvin rushed out from the store to stop them. News had at that minute come of the presence in the neighborhood of eighteen Kiowas said to have escaped recently from the reservation under the leadership of the hostile warrior Sun-Bow. But the boys were not impressed. A few Indians, more or less, only added zest to the situation. So, with thanks and a flourish of new Stetsons, they rattled off up the trail.

Lide's heart sank as she came to a full realization of her plight. With the horses gone, there was no possible means of escape. Besides, no place of safety was close enough to be reached. There she was, one lone woman on a prairie surrounded by savages, the sole protector of two halfgrown girls and a toddling child. She hastened to the creek, then, having gathered her brood together, returned to the house to barricade them as best she could against whatever evil was about to befall.

After that, nothing remained but to watch and hope and pray. Through the endless hours of the day that followed she waited, never stirring from the children's side except now and then to peer with terrified eyes through an opening as she waited in vain for help. But no human or animal form broke the serenity of the landscape. Outside, as within, all was perfectly quiet—not a sound, not a movement—only the ominous swaying of the long grasses as they moved with the wind.

It was well on toward sundown when Corvin rode in. Although he accepted the account of the morning with calm, he took the peaceful day as an unfavorable sign. Most probably the savages with customary wile had lain hidden all the while awaiting the fall of night.

He refused to consider Lide's plea that they make an effort to reach the nearest white neighbors at the R-Two headquarters. One horse was of small use to five people and, once afoot in the open, they were truly at the mercy of the foe. As for his being able to hold out long against the concerted efforts of a band—that, too, he knew to be a feat beyond the accomplishment of one man. Their only chance of survival lay in strategy. The attack must not take place.

Having settled upon a plan, he took himself out into the open where, as long as daylight made his movements visible to the interested onlooker, he appeared busy with the regular afternoon chores. The affairs of the household moved on serenely. Much fuel was gathered, and smoke from the chimney rose high as if in welcome to expected visitors.

But, upon the descent of darkness, all pretense was abandoned, and the family made haste to creep toward the refuge of a grove of trees that grew on the river bank a half-mile away. There, through the night, they waited and waited. When dawn finally broke and the fearful shadows around them scattered before the sun's lengthening rays, the five emerged from hiding to trudge sleepily back to the house, thoroughly ashamed of a procedure that, by the light of day, appeared cowardly and lacking in loyalty to the Indians who had previously proved friendly to them.

Nevertheless, their premonitions had not been far wrong. At noon a scouting party of soldiers arrived to announce that after a hard chase the fugitives had been captured, but not in time to prevent some heinous deeds. The marauders had run across the two boys on the first night after the youngsters' departure from the store, and, having surprised them as they sat around their campfire, killed one outright and left the other to die. However, he did not die but lived to tell of his experience and to show as proof of the tale the bald spot acquired when he was scalped by the enemy. Later, when questioned, the Indians admitted that an attack on the settlement had been planned but was abandoned because of the suspected presence of buffalo hunters, with whom experience had taught the Indians not to interfere. Corvin's assumed composure was probably the gesture that saved the day.

Other than this one time, there was little occasion for fear, and the store prospered and grew. In 1881, the picket house was made the warehouse, and roomier quarters of adobe were built for business purposes. Two additional log cabins were erected, one for Corvin's family and the other for Jonathan's, an arrangement that at the time was the height of luxury.

By 1887, the store required even more space, and a larger frame building was constructed of lumber hauled from Gainesville. As Doan's was at the time the largest supply station for those traveling to Kansas by way of the Panhandle, everything was bought and sold in quantity.

Commodities like flour, grain, and bacon were purchased by the carload, then freighted by wagons from the rail terminus. There were also Stetson hats, cartridges, rifles, six-shooters, and the many other items of common use on the frontier. A generous supply of medicine was always on hand, with quinine and calomel prescribed as the cure for most maladies. Credit was extended to all, and never a dollar was lost.

As others moved in to join the first family, the settlement grew, until at its height it numbered over a hundred inhabitants and boasted twelve houses, among them a saloon, a wagonyard, a hotel called the "Bat's Cave," and the post office, over which Uncle Cal presided, guarding with special care any missive addressed in a feminine hand to an eager but bashful cowboy.

Although the men were a rough lot and there was much drinking and shooting, there was never a murder. Jonathan composed a committee of one to enforce the law, being at first self-appointed but later retaining his position by popular consent. It was at this time that he came to be called "the Judge."[4] When a man became obstreperous, the "walking and talking" system was employed, to be succeeded, in case of failure, by the sterner method of

4 Jonathan Doan was Wilbarger County's first elected judge.

Additional Facts, Figures, and Stories 155

dropping the trouble-stirring fellow into an abandoned well where, in the absence of a calaboose, he was allowed to remain until sober and subject to reason.

About fifteen miles to the south was Eagle Flat (later called Vernon) with its two families, grocery store, and beer saloon, the roundup ground where the trail herds were bedded down or reshaped before crossing the Red River and entering the Indian Territory.

There were always weeks of preparation in the spring before the outfits began to come. Lide unpacked her cashmere shawl, the sewing machine ran constantly, and bright ribbons were ordered to wear to the dances that took place nearly every night. Young Eva Doan was the beauty with her long black curls, big brown eyes, and quiet ways, and it was for her favors the men vied until the day Bud Braziel came along.

The trail cutters, who arrived in advance of the others, held the most enviable job, as their work necessitated their remaining at the crossing during the entire season so as to be on hand to reclaim from passing cattle any stray marked with their boss's brand. During these times, the herds followed, one close upon the heels of the others, and the settlement teemed with activity.

Thus, with Indians, roistering cowboys, brave women, and a law all its own the little store flourished and grew

as the longhorns moved out upon the Panhandle's waiting plains.

Various Ranches in the South of the Panhandle

Forming the western, southern, and eastern boundaries of the Quarter Circle Heart were the fences of the Bar O (later the Half Circle K), Diamond F, JA, Spade, and RO outfits, and to the north was open range. Away to the south on the Red River were the Diamond Tail, Mill Iron, and Shoe Bar.

The JA story has already been told, and that of the Shoe Bar and Mill Iron is a well-known matter of history, mentioned here only because of the fact that in their early life the two absorbed the famous Rockingchair and Shoe Nail brands. In 1879, L. G. Coleman came from Colorado to locate upon the Red River where, in partnership with Leigh Dyer, he started the Shoe Bar Ranch. In 1883, the property was sold to their manager, Judge O. H. Nelson, and T. S. Bugbee, who had recently disposed of the Quarter Circle T to the Prairie Land and Cattle Company. Some time later, Swift and Company bought both the Shoe Bar and Shoe Nail outfits and merged them under the brand of the former. In 1911, all the cattle and the land lying to the south of the Red River went into the hands of W. J. Lewis, and it is now the property of Mrs. W. J. Lewis, Jr.

Although the colony was the Shoe Bar outfit's point of trade, the ranch has little connection with this narrative. But it is of interest because Leigh Dyer was a brother of Mrs. Goodnight and because Judge Nelson was responsible for the presence of Hereford cattle in the Panhandle.

In the early 1860's, Noah Ellis began branding a few head of cattle down in South Texas with the Rocking-chair brand. After a time, he moved to the Panhandle, locating on Elm Creek, not far from the present town of Shamrock. Ellis was a free grass stockman and, accordingly, owned very little land, but, whatever the amount, he sold it along with his herd sometime close to 1880 to an English syndicate of which John Drew was the manager. Now, it so happened that the aggregate holdings of the company covered about two-thirds of Collingsworth County and that Collingsworth lay next to Greer, a county which, because of its location, was later included in Oklahoma but was at that time an isolated Texas district surrounded on three sides by the Indian Territory—an easy point of entry and egress for the neighboring desperadoes. As a result, Collingsworth became infested with rustlers whose successful activities doomed to failure the companies attempting to ranch within its boundaries.

Drew was an eastern man, in no way competent to manage the affairs of a ranch so situated. Consequently, between one kind of loss and another, the business failed to prosper. By the time "Cap" Arrington was put in charge, the company was too weakened financially to be revived even by so seasoned a veteran as "the ranger captain," and the only recourse was to close it out. The cattle were shipped, and the land was sold to Colonel W. W. Hughes and Colonel John Simpson to become a part of their extensive Mill Iron outfit.

In 1882, Thomas Richards and J. W. Sacra bought and patented 31,000 acres of land that they might wedge in between the large ranges of the Diamond F and the Quarter Circle Heart a small ranch called the Bar O. Soon Richards sold his half to E. C. and J. W. Sugg. About 1884, they sold out to Bill Koogle, who, with the consent of his partners, Ralph Jefferson and Charles J. Lewis, changed the brand to the Half Circle K.

The outfit was comparatively small, but, if it were possible to tell of its rise and fall in terms of human equations rather than in the more prosaic manner of dates and figures and facts, it would constitute a complete social history of the West, for in the varied successes and tragedies of the owners lay a story of Indians and desperadoes and cattle kings, of brave women and weak men, of transplanted gentlefolk, and of a boy who arose from the wreckage of blasted hopes to build a fortune and add honor to an already worthy name.

Bill Koogle was an adventurer by nature. Having come at last in his peregrinations to a rough and ready region suited to his taste, he became first a buffalo hunter in Kansas, then a bullwhacker in Texas, then a fencing contractor, and finally a cattleman. Like the land around him, he expressed himself by extremes. When he drove a team, it was a team of eight oxen yoked as one; when he hunted, it was in pursuit of the mighty buffalo; when he contracted, it was to enclose a virgin land with barbed wire; when he married, his bride was the most beautiful girl of his acquaintance and one of the belles of Kansas City; when he traveled, it was by private Pullman car; when he ranched, it was in the manner of all free grass barons; and, when he reached the end of his western career, that, too, he closed with fitting drama.

The Sugg brothers were men of the same character. Although they operated all over the Southwest, it is with the Indian Territory that their name is most commonly associated. Their range was huge and their cattle many; their feudal domain was an absolute monarchy ruled by the iron hand of an outfit of fighting men.

Ralph Jefferson was a dilettante, reared in the atmos-phere of the national capital's best society, a linguist, an amateur actor of no mean ability, and a generally pleasant fellow, too convivially inclined to be concerned with finance or any other business of a serious nature.

Charlie Lewis was a merchant, scholarly, unaggressive, conscientious, and entirely lacking in the qualities most necessary to the life of the frontier. What sardonic humor caused fate, by a brand, to bind into one unit men of such dissimilar background, character, and purpose?

Lying directly across the Heart range on the opposite side was the Spade Ranch, small in size also but of much importance as the forerunner of a brand still famous today. The founder, J. F. Evans, was a cattleman from Sherman. In some way he became associated with J. P. Warner, co-agent with H. B. Sanborn for the sale of barbed wire in Texas. Evans, accustomed to crossing the region with his trail herds, was attracted to the Panhandle because of its advantages as a range, and Warner because of its suitability to the uses of the commodity he was exploiting.

On August 25, 1880, they purchased from J. A. Reynolds the first of the twenty-three sections that were to become the Spade Ranch. They had collected a herd in Lamar County, branded it according to the suggestion of Dave Cummings, a friend of Evans, and then trailed it to the long grasses of the Panhandle. The cattle were turned loose on the Sadler Creek, but camp was established on the Glenwood. Later a log house was built on the Barton Creek, and permanent headquarters were established there. As Evans's other interests required much of his attention, he spent little time in the West, leaving the active management to such men as Dave Nall and Baldy Oliver.

In the same year that Evans located in Donley, one J. Taylor Barr established headquarters near Renderbrook Springs in Mitchell County. Two years later, D. H. and J. W. Snider, having bought him out, enlarged the outfit to include 130,000 acres of land to which, by the purchase in 1882 of a ranch on the South Plains, was added another 128,000 acres.

In December, 1888, Evans sold out to Isaac L. Ellwood, co-owner with J. F. Glidden of the barbed-wire patent. Some few months later, the northern operator also purchased the South Plains Renderbrook Ranch, to which range he transferred his recently acquired Spade herd and brand. In 1891, he took over the remaining Renderbrook holdings, thus giving the new Spade Ranch a range of some 275,000 acres.

To the east of the narrow strip of land that was once the original Spade range lay the 60,000 acres of fertile, rolling prairies known as the RO Ranch, a ranch closely associated both with the colony and with the new Clarendon which the colony later became. Across the ranch's southern extremity, the Salt Fork still runs and in its draws each spring thousands of mother cows and their calves still seek refuge from the cold and graze upon the grasses that grow along the banks of the river's numerous tributary creeks.

The RO's second owner, W. J. Lewis, was a son of the colony whose first cowboy job with pay was as "outside man" for the outfit. Its first owner was Alfred Rowe, an Englishman who succeeded where others of his countrymen failed because of his ability to abandon the Britisher's innate snobbery and to simulate the ways of democracy, at least while in America. Men like Goodnight laid the foundation upon which a new West was to arise. Men like White gave birth to its spirit, and men like Rowe nurtured that spirit into a leaven that altered the character of the entire frontier.

Exactly how he happened into the Panhandle is not known, but, as the woman he later married was the niece of Charles Kingsley, and as James Hughes, whose father was also a famous writer, sold Rowe his first herd of cattle, it is probable that through personal acquaintances or friends abroad an Englishman already successfully established in the Panhandle influenced the one at home to migrate. Like most boys of the class to which he belonged in England, Alfred Rowe, although reared with all the advantages of wealth, education, and travel, found himself upon reaching manhood deprived both of a livelihood and an occupation by the British custom of bequeathing to the eldest son the family fortune and business. Ranching was not only a gentleman's way of working but a sporting life that intrigued his interest.

He arrived in Donley the year following the founding of the colony and through the purchase of scrip established himself to the north on Skillet Creek. There in a two-room sod house covered with shingles freighted in from Dodge City he set up his first headquarters. Having started his herd with some longhorns trailed up from South Texas by Hughes and McCormick and Joe Horn and having installed as foreman Green McCullum, one of Goodnight's men lent to him as a favor, he set about adding to the land already acquired.

The next purchase was the Whitefish country, which was bought from Carhart and Sully. On the day on which the sale was made, a prophetic incident occurred. The weather was hot, and the buggy ride had been long and wearing—not a propitious introduction to any country. Having arrived at last upon the crest of the hill beyond which lay the creek, Rowe took one long look at his sur-roundings, so unfavorable by comparison to the verdant landscape of the land from which he had come, then re-marked, "This appears to be a very hard country to me," to which the ever-ready Carhart replied, "True, my friend, true, but just think of the scope."

So Alfred looked again and caught the vision of the vast, broad land, and his fortune was made. Although he actually owned approximately the same acreage as that included in the ranch today, through usage of the public domain and leases he at one period controlled a range about thirty miles square, reaching from east of the Rock-ledge switch in Gray County to a little place called Lelia on the north and from there to the present town of Quail and to within five miles of Clarendon. Besides a perma-nent herd of a thousand cows there were four or five thousand steers fattened for shipment each spring.

Sometime later, Alfred was joined by his two broth-ers, Bernard and Vincent, who bought between them a one-third interest in the outfit, which, however, they re-turned to the founder in 1900. Bernard's connection with a chemical factory in Kansas City necessitated his residence there. Vincent did spend much time on the ranch and he took an active part in its management. However, from beginning to end it was Alfred who was the motivating force behind its success.

The three brothers had only one thing in common—their heritage of name and blood. In appearance, manner, and character they bore slight resemblance. Bernard was a meticulous master of detail. During the period in which the books were under his supervision, he added materially to the work of the manager, as all other operations ceased when the figures refused to balance or one item was posted in error. He was known to work for three days at a time over a discrepancy of no more than five cents.

Although Vincent liked the ranch and the West, his real interest lay in things of another nature. It was his lifelong ambition, and one which probably would have been achieved had he lived some years longer, to occupy a seat in the English Parliament. As a result he was given to using on occasion the kind of oratory he hoped to employ in later years—a habit that gave rise to some very amusing incidents.

As he rode into headquarters late one afternoon, he noticed that since his last observation a "nester" had moved in to squat upon an unusually good piece of land near McCormick Creek. To a man as respectful of the law as the Britisher, it was inconceivable that anyone should so openly attempt to appropriate that which belonged to another. He meditated on the matter long and seriously and, having arrived at the conclusion that only ignorance could

have prompted such a deed, seated himself after supper to compose the peroration by which means the offender was to be introduced to matters of the law and individual property rights. All night he worked, arousing first one member of the household and then another from slumber to listen while he recited the words. By morning he was letter perfect, so, in company with the manager, he started in the direction of the scene of dispute. The nester answered his call at once and stood most respectfully as Vincent proclaimed in his best manner a speech that ended to the effect that "you cannot do this thing. The land is mine by law, and if you willfully appropriate it for personal use, you will be taking that to which you have no right and in doing so will be desecrating every principle for which our ancestors fought and bled." And having delivered himself satisfactorily, he touched the horse with the whip and drove off.

The next day the nester, to the surprise of everyone but Vincent, moved on. When asked what reason he had given for submitting so peaceably, a cowboy who had seen him depart said, "Oh, he didn't give much reason at all—just said as he rode off that if Vincent's pappy had fought and bled over that there piece of land, he kind of believed the kid ought to have it."

Alfred, unlike Vincent, did not take his surroundings

quite so seriously. Because of his adaptability, his business principles, and his pleasant manner, he won the affection and respect of cowboy and stockman alike. He was typical of the aristocratic class of Englishmen most prevalent in the West during that period. His dignity, his sense of responsibility, his business code, his interest in the community and in those less fortunate than he, his willingness to work, and his enjoyment of living were mighty influences upon all who lived within the circle of his acquaintance.

About 1894, Rowe bought the Edgell place. The two-room house already there was enlarged into a comfortable, rambling cottage of nine rooms, furnished in the English manner with good, solid furniture, hunting prints, and fine old clocks. When it became headquarters, additional corrals, sheds, barns, and a bunkhouse were built, and there through the years after the coming of new Clarendon lived the British cowman and his boys.

Rowe did not marry until late in life. On one occasion, when questioned on the subject, he tartly replied that he saw no reason to hurry as his father had stayed single till he was forty-seven, in spite of which he had managed to raise a family of seven children.

After the sinking of the *Titanic* on which Alfred was returning from a visit in England, the ranch was placed under the general supervision of W. H. Patrick, who, with the assistance of the foreman, Gregory, continued in charge until 1917, when the outfit was purchased by W. J. Lewis. After Lewis's death, the ranch was divided. Only a part of it remains in the hands of the family. The remainder has recently been sold.

There were many other famous ranches in the Panhandle, but, since they lay to the east, west, or north of Amarillo, they played no part in this story.

COWBOY NAMES

Among the following will be found the names of the men who contributed toward the development of the Panhandle today.

Heart Outfit

Joe Allison	Arch Bryant
Tom Arlington	Jim Buchanan
Jeff Bailey	Bob Byrd
Red Beard	Stuart Campbell
George Beauman	Ed Carhart
Dan Blaylock	Burns Clark, cook
Will Boggs	Johnny Clark
Bill Brooks	Joe Cupell

John Davis
Tom Davis
Nat Erwin
Frank Groves
Alex Gugg
Jack Hall, bookkeeper
Gus Hartman, cook
Charlie Heisler
Harve Howe
Ed Johnson
John Kent
Ed Kinsington
Jeff Layton
Charlie Lottinsdale
Tom Martindale
Herbert Mathewson
Dave Maxwell
Mexican José
Homer Mills
James Moore
Gene Mosher
Frank Mulkins
Dan Nall
Ed Nall
Negro Bob, cook

Negro Henry, cook
C. M. O'Donel, manager
George Owen
Jack Owen
Wally Parks
Henry Phillips
Roscoe Philpot, wagon boss
Hoyt Robertson, the "Heart Kid" (which means "the youngest")
Charley Shelton
Hank Stanton
Tom Strange
George Strong
John Stubblefield
Henry Taylor, manager
Frank Wall
Louis Webb
Sid Webb
Tommy White, ranger
Archie Williams
Jim Williams
Charley Wright
Jesse Wynne

Diamond Tail Outfit

Johnnie Arnold
Jim (Pie-biter) Baker, cook and storekeeper
Reece Barton, trail boss
Jim Barnes, wagon boss
Sam Bean
Charlie Beverly
Sid Davidson
Elmo Dodson
John Dodson
Bill Ellis
Town Embree, wagon boss
Scott (Six-Shooter) Ferguson
Giles Flippen, wagon boss
Frank Gallagher

Hick Garrison
J. W. Garrison
Al Gentry
Pat Gharmley, trail boss
John Holman, trail boss
Mexican George, horse wrangler
Baldy Oliver
W. S. Pitts
Billie Smith, wagon boss
W. C. Stone
George Weckes, wagon boss
Ben Wolforth
George Wolforth
Pat Wolforth, wagon boss

Spade Outfit

George Berry
Bill Fleck
Frank Groves
Bob McJemsey
Al McKinney
Homer Mills

Bob Nall
Frank Nall
Tom Strange
Steve Taylor
Charlie Wright

Rowe Outfit

Charlie Beverly, manager	Bob Muir
Will Beverly, manager	Will Muir
Jim Chrystal, manager	Baldy Oliver
Henry Crawford, bronc-buster	George Overrocker
	—— Peachry, manager
Buster Culdwell	Clint Phillips
—— Gregory, manager	—— Potts
—— Henderson, manager	—— Richardson
Henry Hodge, wagon boss	Dayton Shelton
Billey Humphrey	Bob Sowder
W. J. Lewis	Jasper Stevens
George Lynch	Tom Strange
Tom McCarty, well-driller	Wiley Vinson
D. S. McClellan	—— Vinson
John McClellan	John Wagner, bronc-buster
Lew McClellan	Monroe Wagner
John McCormick	Everett Watkins
Green McCullum, manager	Pole West, manager
Billy McMaster	Joe Williams, manager
Charlie McMurtry	—— Wilson, manager
John Molesworth, manager	Dan Zachary

Also, J. W. Kent, possibly for a little while, and Joe Horn (who was never a member of the outfit but always worked through with them at branding time be-cause Alfred said he was the only man in the Panhandle who could throw a calf without injuring it).

PANHANDLE FIRSTS

The First Thoroughbred Cattle

"In a study of the early history of registered Herefords in the Panhandle the name of Judge O. H. Nelson . . . is met with frequently . . . his entrance into the Hereford business in Texas was not in the capacity of a breeder of registered cattle but as a dealer in bulls. He was a member of the firm of Finch, Lord and Nelson of Burlingame, Kansas. In the spring of 1883 (some say earlier) Nelson purchased between 500 and 600 head of young cows and 20 bulls . . . located on a ranch . . . near where Tulia is now situated . . . the bulls cost Nelson $300 to $600 a head. Later the same year he sold the herd to Goodnight. . . . bulls all registered Herefords . . . most of the cows were shorthorns, but a few were one-half to three-quarters Hereford . . . became the foundation of the famous J. J. and J. A. commercial herds."[5]

The First Wire Fences

The first wire fence was a "drift fence" built in 1882

[5] John M. Hazleton in *Amarillo Globe News*.

along the northern part of the JA ranch by Henry Taylor and Bill Koogle.[6]

The First Doctor

"Dr. Henry [F.] Hoyt was born on a Minnesota farm . . . [and] took up the study of medicine in a doctor's office in St. Paul in 1874. To earn his way through college practiced medicine in Deadwood, Dakota Territory, during the summer of 1877. In the fall he went to the Panhandle, said to be the first doctor to practice in this district. In 1881 he returned East to college . . . graduated in 1882 . . . [and] became the chief surgeon of the Great Northern and Chicago and the Burlington Railroad."[7]

The First Banker

"Judge J. C. Paul . . . was born in Virginia in 1852 . . . graduated from the University of Illinois, after going West at the age of twenty . . . farmed for several years . . . moved to Wichita, Kansas, to enter the real estate business . . . became connected with the building of the Southern Kansas into the Panhandle.

"In 1887 moved to Panhandle (Carson) City as treasurer of the railroad and established the first bank in the Panhandle with (G. A. P. Parker) and a capital of two or three thousand dollars."[8]

The First White Child

"My husband and I came to the Panhandle in December, 1875, and built us a two-roomed house on Gageby Creek . . . came from Colorado with a hunting party headed by my husband . . . hired four other men. I would go along and cook for the men, load ammunition, help stake the buffalo hides and sometimes skin them. I enjoyed the camp very much. When the buffalo would get scarce, we would go back to our house . . . 9 miles from Fort Elliott. My son, Joseph, was born there in 1877, *the first child born in the Panhandle.* The officers' wives would come out from the fort every week to see and visit him. They seemed to like the first baby."[9]

The First Marriage

"My father, George Simpson, came to the Panhandle in 1875. My mother, Sylvania Wood, came the same year. The Woods and Simpsons were an organized buffalo-hunting party. My parents were married October, 1877, by

[6] Harley True Burton, *A History of the J. A. Ranch,* p. 93.
[7] *A Frontier Doctor,* by Henry F. Hoyt, introduction.

[8] B. B. Paddock, ed., *A Twentieth Century History and Biographical Record of North and West Texas,* I, 279–280.
[9] Mrs. I. D. (Emily) Wood to author, April 1, 1938, Lewis Papers, Archives, Dallas Historical Society.

Lieut. Taylor at Ft. Elliott, the first marriage in the Panhandle."[10] Whether it was a civil service is not known. It is said, however, that there was a chapel of sorts at the post and always a resident chaplain.

The First Christian Services

(1) "Rev. John Padilla, chaplain to Coronada, offered the first mass in Texas, 40 miles west of Amarillo, near Tascosa, on Ascension Thursday, 1541. . . . he was martyred some place in the Texas Panhandle or close to Herring, Kansas by Indians in 1542 or '43."[11]

(2) Long before the organization of the first Methodist church in Mobeetie (which, according to Mrs. W. R. [Lulu F.] Ewing was a result of the efforts of Professor and Mrs. Boles, Judge Willis's maternal grandparents and Mr. and Mrs. Seiber and did not occur until 1893) two Methodist circuit riders started to Mobeetie but stopped when they reached Sweetwater Creek, having heard by that time of the wickedness of the town and the reception usually accorded any servant of the Lord who dared to enter. Professor Boles, when told by an amused cowboy of the "preachers who were camping on the outskirts because they were afraid to proceed farther," sought them out. After much persuasion and many promises of protection they were induced to hold service for a few spiritual-minded citizens. Johnny Stroker's dance hall, which was selected as the most convenient place for the meeting, was packed when the time arrived. As a usual preliminary the "hat was passed" and returned to its owners filled to the brim with the silver dollars and five and ten dollar bills of the town's most wicked. A sermon followed, then worship through music. There were no song books, and the congregation, most of them, had never heard a hymn; consequently, the minister's attempts to lead the singing were not very successful. At last a cowboy arose and said he could tell them a song "that was kinder religious, and anyway everybody knew it." And the meeting closed under his direction with:

> "Talk about your good things
>   Talk about your glory,
> When you get to Heaven,
>   You'll sure be hunky-dory,"

resounding from the rafters of the dance hall, as the cowboys with gusto sang the words to the tune of "My Grandfather's Clock."[12]

[10] Mrs. Oscar Moore to author, March 19, 1938, Lewis Papers, Archives, Dallas Historical Society.

[11] Rev. Bartholomew O'Brien to author, 1938, Lewis Papers, Archives, Dallas Historical Society.

[12] Judge Newton P. Willis to author, July 1, 1936, Lewis Papers, Archives, Dallas Historical Society.

Bibliography

Author's Interviews (Lewis Papers, Archives, Dallas Historical Society, Dallas, Texas)

Atterbury, Mrs. S. E., August 2, 1935

Atterbury, Mrs. Will, April 25, 1935

Carhart, Ed. E., April 22, 1935

Carhart, Whitfield, April —, 1935

Chamberlain, Mrs. B. W., undated

Chamberlain, Mrs. Rufus A., undated

Culdwell, William C. (Buster), undated

Curtis, J. O., undated

Dixon, Mrs. Olive King, July 27, 1935

Fleming, William Frank, April 27, 1935

Freeman, Mrs. Hattie, April 20, 1935

Gentry, Mrs. Sella Phillips, March 29, 1938

Godwin-Austin, Mrs. Elizabeth, August 5, 1935

Hall, Mrs. Annie Fleming, April 27, 1935

Hardy, Dr. G. S., March 21, 1938

Henry, John, April 29, 1935

Hobart, T. D., April 20, 1935

Horn, Joe, August 10, 1935

———, March 6, 1938

Huselby, Mark, April 29, 1935

Kilfoil, Mrs. James, July 29, 1935

Lewis, Charles R., undated

Lewis, W. J., February 8, 1936

———, March 16, 1938

Lovett, Henry B., April 29, 1935

McClelland, Mrs. J. B., May 15, 1935

McCormick, Mrs. Mickey, undated

McDonald, Mrs. Jessie Morrow, July 27, 1935

Mitchell, Mrs. Frank, March 10, 1938

Martin, Mrs. Maud, April 10, 1935

Molesworth, John, March —, 1938

Muir, R. H., March 16, 1938

Nies, G. E., August 24, 1935

Patrick, W. H., August 14, 1936

———, October 6, 1936

Rosenfield, Morris, undated

Ross, Mrs. Bertha Doan, June 7, 1935

———, July 20, 1935

Sanders, Marvin, August 6, 1935

Searcy, Mallia Washington, July 30, 1935

Snider, John, March 10, 1938

Stocking, Mrs. J. D., undated

Taylor, Crockett W., August 9, 1935

Tomb, Mrs. J. A., August 3, 1935

Williams, James Ewing, March —, 1938

Willis, Judge Newton P., August 16, 1936

Wynne, Jesse Smith, April 20, 1935

Wynne, Jesse, July 23, 1935

Wynne, J[esse] S[mith], March 16, 1938

Young, Mrs. Jessica Morehead, April 25, 1935

Young, Jessica Morehead, undated.

Since publication of the first edition in 1938, transcripts of the author's interviews with the following persons have been lost:

Bigger, Mrs. Robert
Boeding, Rev. Arnold
Estlack, J. D.
King, Rufus
Newbury, Mrs. Lee
Wrather, William Embrey

Letters to Author (Lewis Papers, Archives, Dallas Historical Society, Dallas, Texas)

Arnot, John, July 20, 1938
————, March 11, 1938
————, March 15, 1938
Beedy, Mrs. A. A., March 19, 1938
Braswell, Sam, March 26, 1938
Brown, J. Birl, June —, 1935
Carhart, E. E., March 15, 1938
————, April 11, 1938
Carhart, Whitfield, October 23, 1936
————, March 15, 1938
Chatelain, Verne E., July 17, 1936
————, August 12, 1936

Cooke, A. K., July 30, 1938
Danglmayr, Rev. A., November 29, 1937
Dorsey, W. H., March 9, 1938
Driscoll, J. I., May 6, 1938
Ewing, Mrs. Lulu F., March 27, 1938
Fiege, C. F., August 29, 1935
Fisk, Charles A., October 13, 1936
Graham, Bertha, August 13, 1935
————, March 22, 1938
Heath, Mrs. Mary Allan, June 15, ——
Hopping, R. C., March 17, 1938

Hulen, John, October 12, 1937
Johnston, C. S., August 16, 1935
Koue, Mary E., April 8, 1938
————, April 11, 1938
McCormick, D. R., March 24, 1938
————, April 6, 1938
McKeown, W. B., March 10, 1938
Mahoney, Msgr. Ph. F., February 5, 1938
May, W. H., April 4, 1938
Moore, Mrs. Oscar, March 19, 1938
Murdock, W. J., July 30, 1935
————, March 17, 1938
O'Brien, Rev. Bartholomew, February 9, 1938
————, March 19, 1938
O'Flaherty, Rev. Edward, January 29, 1938
Peet, W. H., March 22, 1938
Porter, Judge J. R., March 16, 1938

Reed, Rev. Aln (*sic*) R., March 4, 1938
Ross, Mrs. Bertha Doan, July 4, 1936
Sanders, M. V., August 26, 1935
Schmidt, Rev. John Rogg, January 14, 1938
Sheffy, L. F., July 7, 1936
Tenney, S. M., January 18, 1938
Thompson, Frank M., July 15, 1935
————, July 25, 1935
Thompson, W. M., August 16, 1935
Vollmar, Edward R., SJ, April 7, ——
Walker, J. H., October 1, 1936
Willis, Judge Newton P., July 1, 1936
Woffard, Harry, undated
Wood, Mrs. Emily, April 1, 1938

Since publication of the first edition in 1938, letters to the author from the following persons have been lost:

Dyer, Mrs. Minnie E.   White, Clifford
Groves, Frank

Manuscripts

Beverly, Cora. "City of Amarillo." Panhandle-Plains Historical Museum, Canyon, Texas.

Douglas, C. L., "The Raven's Fledgeling."

Harrel, Mrs. Jennie. "First History of Old-Town Amarillo." Scrap Book Case, Amarillo Public Library, Amarillo, Texas

Proceedings

Minutes of the Donley County Commissioners Court, Office of the County Clerk, Donley County Court House, Clarendon, Texas.

Minutes of the North Texas Annual Conference of the United Methodist Church. Birdwell Library, Perkins School of Theology, Southern Methodist University, Dallas, Texas.

Minutes of the Northwest Texas Conference of the United Methodist Church. Birdwell Library, Perkins School of Theology, Southern Methodist University, Dallas, Texas, "Golden Jubilee Addresses of the Presbytery of Dallas, U.S.A." 1878–1928.

Books and Pamphlets

Adair, Cornelia. *My Diary*. Privately printed, 1918.

Adams, Andy. *The Log of a Cowboy*. Boston: Houghton Mifflin Co., 1927.

Adams, James Truslow. *Epic of America*. Boston: Little, Brown, 1931.

Allen, J. A. *The American Bisons, Living and Extinct*. Cambridge: The University Press, 1876.

Barker, Eugene C. *Texas History for High Schools and Colleges*. Dallas: Southwest Press, 1929.

Burns, Walter Noble. *The Saga of Billy the Kid*. New York: Garden City Publishing Co., 1925.

Burton, Harley True. *A History of the J. A. Ranch*. Austin: Von Boeckmann-Jones, 1928.

Carter, Capt. R. G. *On the Border with Mackenzie; or, Winning West Texas from the Comanches*. Washington: Eynon Printing Co., 1935.

Catlin, George, *North American Indians*. Philadelphia: Leary, Stuart, and Co., 1913.

DeShields, James T. *Cynthia Ann Parker: The Story of Her Cature*. St. Louis: Chas. B. Woodard, 1886.

Dick, Everett. *The Sod-House Frontier*. New York: D. Appleton-Century, 1937.

Dobie, J. Frank. *A Vaquero of the Brush Country*. Dallas: Southwest Press, 1929.

———. *The Longhorns*. Boston: Little, Brown and Co., 1941.

Early-Day History of Wilbarger County. Vernon: *The Vernon Times*, 1933.

Ford, Gus, ed. *Texas Cattle Brands*. Dallas: Clyde C. Cockrell, 1936.

Gammel, H. P. N., comp. *Laws of Texas 1822–1897*. 10 vols. Austin: Gammel Publishing Co., 1898.

Haley, J. Evetts. *Charles Goodnight, Cowman and Plainsman*. Boston: Houghton Mifflin Co., 1929.

———. *The XIT Ranch of Texas*. Chicago: Lakeside Press, 1929.

Hodge, Frederick Webb, ed. *Handbook of American Indians North of Mexico*. Bureau of American Ethnology, Bulletin 30. 2 parts. Washington: Government Printing Office, 1912.

Holden, William Curry. *Alkali Trails*. Dallas: Southwest Press, 1930.

Hoyt, Henry F. *A Frontier Doctor*. Boston: Houghton Mifflin Co., 1929.

McClelland, Mrs. J. B. *A History of St. John the Baptist Protestant Episcopal Church at Clarendon, Texas 1887–1936*. Privately published, undated.

McConnell, Joseph Carroll. *The West Texas Frontier*. 2 vols. Jacksboro: Gazette Print, 1933.

Miles, Gen. Nelson A. *Personal Recollections and Observations*. Chicago: Werner, 1896.

Newton, Lewis W., and Herbert P. Gambrell. *A Social and Political History of Texas*. Dallas: Southwest Press, 1932.

Paddock, B. B., ed. *A Twentieth-Century History and Biographical Record of North and West Texas*. 2 vols. Chicago and New York: Lewis Publishing Company, 1906.

Phelan, Macum. *A History of the Expansion of Methodism, 1867–1902*. Dallas: Mathis, Van Nort, 1937.

Richardson, Rupert Norval. *The Comanche Barrier to South Plains Settlement*. Glendale, Calif.: Arthur H. Clark, 1933.

Saunders, Geo. W. *The Trail Drivers of Texas*. Edited by J. Marvin Hunter. Nashville: Cokesbury Press, 1925.

Thompson, James Westfall, and Edgar Nathaniel Johnson. *An Introduction to Mediaeval History*. New York: W. W. Norton, 1937.

Vestal, Stanley. *Mountain Men*. Boston: Houghton Mifflin Co., 1937.

Webb, Walter Prescott. *The Great Plains*. Boston: Ginn and Company, 1931.

Winship, George Parker, trans. and ed. *The Journey of Coronado, 1540–1542*. New York: Allerton, 1922.

Wissler, Clark. *Man and Culture*. New York: Thomas Y. Crowell Co., 1923.

———. *North American Indians of the Plains*. New York: American Museum of Natural History, 1934.

Periodicals

Arnot, John. "My Recollections of Tascosa before and after the Coming of the Law." *Panhandle-Plains Historical Review* 6 (1933).

Carleson, Avis D. "Dust Blowing." *Harper's Magazine* 171 (July, 1935).

Gettinger, Roy. "The Separation of Nebraska and Kansas from the Indian Territory." *Chronicles of Oklahoma* 1, no. 1 (January, 1921).

Haley, J. Evetts. "The Grass Lease Fight and Attempted Impeachment of the First Panhandle Judge." *Southwesern Hisorical Quarterly* 38, no. 1 (July, 1934).

Leckie, William H. "The Red River War, 1874–1875." *Panhandle-Plains Historical Review* 29 (1956).

Officer, Helen Bugbee. "A Sketch of the Life of Thomas Sherman Bugbee: 1841–1925." *Panhandle-Plains Historical Review* 5 (1932).

Parker, G. A. F. "Incipient Trade and Religion in Amarillo during the Late Eighties." *Panhandle-Plains Historical Review* 2 (1929).

Sheffy, L. F. "Old Mobeetie—The Capital of the Panhandle." *West Texas Historical Association Yearbook* 6 (1930).

Stirling, Mathew W. "America's First Settlers, the Indians." *National Geographic Magazine* 72, no. 5 (November, 1937).

"W. J. Murdock Writes of Moving to Old Clarendon in 1881 —Recites Incidents of Early Development." *Clarendon News* (July 4, 1935).

Wardell, M. L. "Southwest's History Written in Oklahoma's Boundary Story." *Chronicles of Oklahoma* 5, no. 3 (September, 1927).

Wellman, Paul I. "Cynthia Ann Parker." *Chronicles of Oklahoma* 12, no. 2 (June, 1934).

West, G. Derek. "The Battle of Adobe Walls (1874)." *Panhandle-Plains Historical Review* 36 (1963).

Index